You Never Know What You Don't Know

The Unwritten Rule of Business from **A** *to* **Z**

Patricia Pitsel, Ph.D.

Suite 300 - 990 Fort St
Victoria, BC, Canada, V8V 3K2
www.friesenpress.com

Copyright © 2015 by Patricia Pitsel, Ph.D.

First Edition — 2015

All rights reserved.

No part of this publication may be reproduced in any form, or by any means, electronic or mechanical, including photocopying, recording, or any information browsing, storage, or retrieval system, without permission in writing from the publisher.

ISBN
978-1-4602-5423-3 (Hardcover)
978-1-4602-5424-0 (Paperback)
978-1-4602-5425-7 (eBook)

1. Business & Economics, Careers

Distributed to the trade by The Ingram Book Company

CONTENTS

INTRODUCTION ... i
A Is For Anger ... 1
B Is For Brains ... 5
C Is For Creativity ... 8
D Is For Defensive ... 13
E Is For Effort ... 18
F Is For Failure ... 22
G Is For Games ... 27
H Is For Humour ... 32
I Is For Indiscretion ... 38
J Is For Judgment ... 42
K Is For Kudos ... 46
L Is For Language ... 50
M Is For Moody ... 54
N Is For Negotiate ... 57
O Is For Office ... 61
P Is For Politics ... 66
Q Is For Qualifications ... 70
R Is For Raises ... 75
S Is For Sex ... 79
T Is For Teamwork ... 83
U Is For Uncertainty ... 87
V Is For Vision ... 93
W Is For Water Cooler ... 97
X Is For Xantippe ... 101
Y Is For Youth ... 106
Z Is For Zombie ... 110
EPILOGUE ... 115

INTRODUCTION

I KNOW THAT EACH GENERATION feels that it has a lock on wisdom, and I don't think that my generation is any different. If there is a difference, however, between the Millennials and the Boomers, it can be summed up thusly: Good judgement is what you get from experience. Experience is what you get from bad judgement.

This book is intended for young professionals who are just now entering the workforce, those who have just been promoted into their first supervisory or management position, or for those who may have been asked to leave a previous job with little idea about why it didn't work out. You see, there are a whole bunch of unwritten rules that are very important, but the people who make these rules never tell you what they are. They just expect that, since to them most are considered to be just common sense, you should know them and obey them as a matter of course.

Work life for many Boomers was uncertain. Because of their numbers and the competition for good jobs, Boomers had to get an edge any way that they could. And now that they are running companies they expect that those who have the "right stuff" will approach work with the same attitudes and understanding of the rules that they had. It really is a classic example of the golden rule: he who has the gold makes the rules.

Most of us, unfortunately, have forgotten that common sense is something that has to be taught and learned. It is not innate. The process seems to go something like this: We learn something and it seems so obvious that we immediately think, "Of course. That's just common sense," and then we forget that there was a time that we did not know it. It's so obvious that everybody must know it, right?

The world would be a much simpler place if that were true, but the unwritten business "rules" identified in this book are culturally and age-dependent. And, hard as it may be to accept, the newest recruit to the organization does not get to make the rules.

Let's consider a simple example. Many North Americans and English think that lining up (queuing) in order of arrival to purchase something just makes sense. It reduces pushing and shoving and allows things to proceed in an orderly fashion so that the strong don't benefit at the expense of the weak. It makes sense, unless, of course, you come from a culture where people do not queue. Lining up for service is a rule that most of us expect our fellow citizens to observe—and we can become quite belligerent if others try to butt into line.

You Don't Know What You Don't Know has been written to provide some food for thought on many of the common rules that are in place in many companies and organizations—private, public, or not-for-profit. Chapters are arranged alphabetically and each chapter covers a specific issue, focusing on an unwritten rule that probably exists where you work. The beginning of each chapter provides an example of a demographically varied team, perhaps much like the group you work with, and a challenge that the various team members face. Following the example, there is a *To Think About* section, which provides a short reflection on why the behaviour was problematic, followed by a *To Do* section, which outlines some strategies that you can use if you find the material pertinent to your situation. The chapters do not have to be read in order, of course. You can pick and choose topics as needed or browse randomly.

I have tried to make the information as practical as possible and the examples real. Most of the examples are real events that I have observed over thirty-plus years of consulting, teaching, and coaching. Some of us can learn from other people's examples, but the rest of us are the other people. While I would love to be able to claim that I have learned from watching all the mistakes that others have made, the truth is that I have made many of the mistakes presented in the following chapters myself. I broke rules that nobody ever told me existed. My sincere wish is that by reading this book you will make fewer mistakes and gain greater wisdom.

Patricia Pitsel, PhD
Calgary, Alberta
2014

A
IS FOR ANGER

Holding onto anger is like drinking poison and expecting the other person to die.
— Buddha

JULIA BARLOW POKED HER HEAD around Lori Johnson's door. The HR Manager of PLP Ltd. was sitting at her desk, staring at the computer screen. "Got a minute?" she asked tightly. She had her reading glasses clutched in one hand and a folder in the other.

"Of course, Julia. You look really steamed. What 's going on?" Lori stood up from behind her desk and moved over to a smaller round table with two chairs. She motioned to Julia. "Please, sit down."

"I just had a screaming match with Jason in our meeting with him and Tom and the marketing group. I totally lost it. It's all his fault. If he hadn't made me so mad I could have solved the whole problem in two minutes. But when he started blaming me for that project going wrong, I...."

"Whoa, Julia—take a deep breath! I can practically see sparks coming off your head."

Julia took a deep breath, slumped down in the chair and stuck her legs straight out in front. "It's not fair," she went on in an only slightly calmer tone. "The men around here just think they can push you and push you until you explode and then you're just a hysterical female. It's not fair and I'm not going to stand for it anymore."

"You sound as if this might have been building for awhile," Lori commented pushing her container of mints closer to Julia.

Julia grabbed a mint and bit down hard. "Well, he had it coming. I can't believe he tried to make me look so bad in front of everyone else."

"Sounds as if he was successful."

"I doubt it! I told him in no uncertain terms that I wasn't there to do his bidding, and that he never, ever offers to help out, and that his own projects are no textbook example of success—never on time and over budget and…." Her voice slowed down as she looked at Lori calmly sitting across from her.

"That's not what you meant is it?" she asked suspiciously. "Are you saying it's my fault? Are you taking his side?" Her voice rose again.

"No, I'm not suggesting that at all and I'm certainly not taking sides. But you said you thought his intent was to make you look bad in front of the rest of the group. How do you think the rest of the group reacted to you and the 'screaming match,' as you phrased it?" Lori sat back and waited for a reply.

TO THINK ABOUT

Whenever I ask adult students in my university classes if they have been in work situations where they have seen an open display of anger, or even fury, nearly all raise their hand. Yet none of them agree that showing this kind of anger accomplishes anything positive. Over and over again in the classes, students describe the person who "loses it" as a bully, undisciplined, and unprofessional.

Are you the type of person who becomes visibly angry when things are not done exactly the way you think they should be—when things are done without your knowledge or permission or when decisions are made that put you or the company at risk? Perhaps your anger boils over when people do things that make you look foolish, inadequate, or incompetent. In short, we don't always get our way, but how you manage your anger quickly becomes known in the organization.

"But what," you might ask, "is the problem with showing my true feelings?" Well, in addition to the obvious consequence of damaging a relationship, perhaps irreparably, there is an additional risk of closing the door to needed information. If you throw a temper tantrum every time someone brings you bad news, the result is that pretty soon no one will tell you anything about the things that need fixing. The result of this may well be that you will be held accountable for things you didn't know were problems in the first place.

While it is true that some corporate leaders have been known for their temper and anger outbursts, no one attributes these outbursts as the cause of their success. They drive away more talent than they attract and create unnecessary hostility where the energy of subordinates can be focused on revenge rather than results. Remember: "You can't talk to someone's head when their heart wants to kill you."

TO DO

Short of enrolling in an anger management class, or holding your breath until you count ver-r-r-y slowly to a thousand, how can you keep your anger in check when you think you have been provoked?

First, keep breathing. The natural response when you feel attacked is to take a breath and then stop breathing. Take deep, even breaths. This will keep you relaxed (as relaxed as you can be under the circumstances) and keep oxygen moving to your brain. As you exhale, think to yourself, "relax."

Second, before responding in an angry fashion to something a person says, repeat the words back, verbatim, but more slowly than originally delivered. Slowing the conversation down will, for most people, reduce the intensity of the feelings.

When you find yourself feeling angry, ask yourself, "How old am I right now?" Am I acting as an emotional child or a rational, mature adult? This question helps you to identify whether you are experiencing what is happening right now or experiencing a feeling from the past when you were much younger. If you had parents who were very critical of you when you were a child, for example, experiencing the critical comments of a supervisor may send you right back, emotionally, to a time when you felt helpless. The anger that you could not express toward your parents now comes rushing out. Asking yourself how old you are now, the instant you feel the anger, interrupts the feeling and allows you to redirect the emotion.

Before you respond to the anger directed at you, get the facts. Find out exactly what the person is talking about and specifically what the complaint is. Is the anger focused on you because you are you or because of something you have done? If it is the latter, find out what is wrong and work on finding a solution rather than defending what you did or explaining why you did it. Explanations are often perceived as defensiveness and may elicit defensiveness in return.

If you are expressing anger use it strategically. Do not yell, scream, shout, cry, threaten, or humiliate people, especially in public. People who have been humiliated, especially in front of others, get even. They may be too professional to sabotage the job, but they may not hesitate to sabotage your reputation in the organization.

Anger also gives energy. Use the anger to get things done, not do people in. Remember that people may invite you to become angry. You don't have to accept the invitation.

B
IS FOR BRAINS

Brains are an asset if you hide them."
— *Mae West*

"IT'S NOT THAT I DON'T like bright young guys," Frank Tarnowski said slowly.

"But don't you think you're overdoing it?"

"What do you mean 'overdoing it'?" Jason McKay asked, grabbing a bottle of water from the lunchroom fridge.

"Well, for one thing, quoting all those studies and stuff you said you read about in school. It sounds as if you think we're all a bunch of dummies here."

Jason's face reddened as he turned toward Frank. "I was just trying to show you guys how to do it better. We studied this type of situation in my MBA marketing classes, exactly the same type of thing, and I don't want to see PLP making the same mistakes they did in the case study."

"That's exactly what I mean," said Frank. "It's MBA this, MBA that, professor this and some guru that. Quit sucking up to the boss and trying to show up the rest of us. We may not have a new fancy MBA behind our name and on our office wall, but we've been in this business a hell of a lot longer than you have. And I bet none of those magic men you quote all the time have ever run a real business. This is the real world, Jason, not some B-school project."

Frank abruptly strode out of the coffee room, leaving Jason standing by the fridge, bottle in hand.

TO THINK ABOUT

A surprising number of people equate brains with academic credentials. It is very useful to have credentials, but it's just not very useful to brag about them or to use them as a power play to be one up on your colleagues.

While it is true that a certain type of intelligence is required to be successful in achieving academic success, the opposite is not necessarily true. It does not follow that people who have not selected an academic route are somehow deficient in the brains department.

Unfortunately, most of us develop ideas about our brains, or lack thereof, by the time we have finished grade one. That assessment is based on a pretty narrow view of what it means to have brains, to be smart, or to be considered intelligent.

If by "brains" we mean the ability to learn theoretical and abstract concepts, then brains are highly over-rated in business. We have seen all sorts of so-called intelligent people without ethics, resulting in scandals on Wall Street, intelligent people without compassion, resulting in an increasing level of disability leave due to stress, and intelligent people without social skills, resulting in technical geniuses who can't communicate their ideas or sell their products to customers. It isn't that good average intelligence is not important, but people who think that they should be promoted or listened to just because they have a piece of paper with a little gold seal on it aren't as smart as they need to be.

The types of brain power that predict success in the business world involves such types of intelligence as knowing how to read people and structure solid relationships, the ability to solve problems and set and achieve goals, and perhaps most important, knowing when to call in an "expert" in any area, including your own, to make use of highly specialized skills. The people who have the brains to manage these kinds of challenges have little need to publicly promote their brainpower. The results speak for themselves.

TO DO

Before you post your diplomas and certificates on the wall, check the other offices to see what your peers do. If they put theirs up, then you should too. Check business cards of people in your industry. Is it common practice to include professional designations, degrees, or certifications?

Where is your industry and profession heading in terms of entry credentials? If all the young people coming into your industry or profession have academic credentials, you may have to upgrade your training in order to stay competitive.

Don't confuse credentials with brains and don't base your estimate of how successful you will be in business on your academic success. And don't stay out of post-secondary education because you weren't the class Einstein in high school. Higher education can bring out the best in all who pursue it.

C
IS FOR CREATIVITY

Go and make interesting mistakes, make amazing mistakes, make glorious and fantastic mistakes. Break rules. Leave the world more interesting for your being here. Make. Good. Art.
— Neil Gaiman

JASON, AS USUAL, WAS THE first one out of the gate with some new ideas on improving PLP promotion and advertising. As Marketing Manager he was responsible for coming up with a new promotional campaign that would increase their market share in the local area.

"My plan," he said to the group assembled for their weekly meeting, "is to skip my usual report and instead take some time to brainstorm some ideas for our new promotion campaign."

"Jason, I thought you were going to bring your ideas to this meeting, not have us do your work for you," Julia said, annoyance clearly evident in her tone.

"I don't know anything about marketing or promotions," Norman Lui, the newly appointed Chief Accountant offered quickly, hoping to defuse Julia's remark. "So I'm not sure that there is much I can add to a discussion. However, if you do need some data or numbers, I'm sure that I can get my staff to pull them up and run them through a quick analysis and see whether they are within our budget forecast."

"Come on folks," COO Tom Arnold broke in. "Let's give young Jason here some help and work together as a team. Surely some of you have some good ideas as to how we can promote our services in this local area. Jason, why don't you kick off the brainstorming by giving us one of your ideas?"

"Well," Jason replied, "I thought we could hire a major celebrity to do a TV spot for us and show it over the local cable company."

"We don't have the budget for that," Norman replied matter-of-factly.

"We tried that before about ten years ago," Frank, added, "and nobody watched it—and our sales certainly didn't go up as a result. We didn't get one new customer."

"How about giving away a computer game to anyone booking with us from now until Christmas?" Karim Hassan, the IT Manager, suggested.

"That won't work," Lori said. "Our female clients probably don't play computer games. And besides, if we don't have the money for a celebrity we certainly don't have the budget for computer games to give away."

The group grew silent.

"Well then," said Tom, "if no one has any more good ideas, why don't we move on to the next report. Julia?"

TO THINK ABOUT

There is probably nothing in business that is praised more but which is practised less than creativity. When organizations ask me to work on creativity with them, the first question I ask is, "How do you reward failure?"

"Don't you mean success?" they correct.

"No," is my response. "It is easy to celebrate and reward success. What is hard, but essential, is to reward failure because that demonstrates that you really value creativity in your organization. Very few creative ideas are successful immediately. They have to be refined, shaped, and worked on."

Few people actually come out and say, "Do what you're told. When I want your opinion, I'll give it to you." No one says, "Keep doing all the old, stupid things, in the old, stupid ways." Yes, often that is how some companies actually run their organizations.

There are few things that threaten companies more than being told they have to be creative because creativity implies risk, the possibility of failure, and the certainty of change.

"If it ain't broke, don't fix it," "We've never done this before," 'It can't be done,'" "Things are going fine as they are,"—all of these comments present formidable blocks to creative thinking and action. Sometimes throwing out creative ideas in a meeting is like being on a duck hunt. As soon as the idea is tossed out, somebody yells, "Duck," and immediately everyone in the group raises their shotgun and tries to blast it out of the air.

TO DO

Creativity needs thinking and reflective time, so if you keep people super busy with all sorts of little, disjointed tasks, you help make sure that they don't have time to come up with creative solutions to old problems—and even more important, creative solutions for problems that can't be solved using the old ways. In his classic *The Practice of Management*, well-known management consultant Peter Drucker (1909-2005) refers to the "activity trap," the state of thinking everything is going well as long as everyone is busy doing something.

Creativity has as much to do with risk taking as it does with originality. How can you encourage creativity in your area? Reward risk taking, even if it doesn't work out well. It's easier to focus on someone who has some wild ideas than to produce ideas in someone who is used to walking the route with blinders.

When someone comes to you with an idea to which your first response is, "That's stupid, it will never work," ask for more information, more details, what problem they are trying to solve, or for a demonstration. You see, no one comes to you with an idea that is really stupid with the motive of seeing whether they'll make the top ten list of stupid people in the company. They have an idea that to them, at least, has some merit. Before you reject it, make sure you understand it. Perhaps part of it is salvageable!

How can you improve your ability to be more creative? The most obvious thing is to start by doing one new or different thing every single day—record it, write down how you felt about it, and, if you like, record the results. It can be something as insignificant as wearing your watch on your other arm, trying a different type of restaurant for lunch, or watching a wrestling match on TV when you'd prefer Masterpiece Theatre.

Before you do something the old or comfortable way, ask yourself, "Could I do this in a better way?

Read outside of your professional area. Ask yourself if there is something that is done in another area, another industry, or another culture that could be adapted to your situation.

Don't associate with negative people who make their living out of telling you why things can't or won't work. Remember that the people who tell you that something can't be done are usually standing in the way of those who are doing it. If you have negative people on your team, consider not bringing them into brainstorming situations at the beginning. Rather, use their considerable analytical abilities to refine and strengthen new ideas at a later stage in the creative process. Negative people are great at pointing out the flaws, so often it is a matter of the timing of their input.

That being said, be prepared to work on your own, to spend some, perhaps even a lot of time, thinking and reflecting. Try spending some time without the radio, the tape, the CD. Put your phone on call forward and a sign on your door, such as, "Thinking – only interrupt in an emergency when fast action is required!"

Think of yourself and describe yourself as creative. If you describe yourself as "not-creative," you both limit yourself and give yourself permission not to engage in the strenuous effort of thinking. Be like the Red Queen who told Alice that she thought of several impossible things every day.

And finally, ask yourself, who is going to judge whether or not you are creative? Usually the people who judge you have not been very creative in their own lives—that's why they have time to judge others. Those who are highly creative are usually supportive and encouraging because they know the process and what it takes to turn out creative material. The butcher who prepares the horsemeat is not a producer of a champion thoroughbred.

D
IS FOR DEFENSIVE

It's often a bad sign when people defend themselves against charges which haven't been made.
— Christopher Hitchens

TOM WALKED DOWN THE HALL briskly, his familiar file folder tucked underneath his arm. Spotting Norman, he made an abrupt left turn and cut him off at the cross corridor. Tom was sure that Norman had made a serious error on the figures he had given to him. Pulling him over to an open doorway, Tom outlined his concerns to Norman, both about the accuracy of the figures and the conclusions Norman had made at the end of the report.

The response was unexpected. Norman's hand began to shake as he took the papers from Tom. His tone became intense and Tom was taken aback when Norman began to explain every line to justify the data he had provided. Surprised at this show of emotion and defensiveness, Tom took a step back into the office and Norman pressed forward, becoming more and more agitated. Not only did Norman justify every figure he had included, he bitterly reproached others in the company who did not seem to care about accuracy and how difficult it was to even get them to submit their numbers in a timely fashion.

Tom finally lost patience with what he saw as Norman's unwillingness to accept any responsibility for the report's errors. Thrusting the entire file into Norman's hands, he stopped Norman's ongoing explanation with a sharp word and a dismissive wave of his hand telling him that to revise the figures as a negative variance was not acceptable and to have the revised report on his desk by the end of the day. As he stepped around Norman and made his way back to his own office, Tom felt a pang of remorse about the harsh tone he had used, but if there was one thing he couldn't tolerate from his team it was excuses.

TO THINK ABOUT

One of the most difficult tasks for many managers is giving critical or negative feedback. It's even more difficult when the person receiving the feedback becomes defensive, hostile, argumentative, and unwilling to rationally consider the criticism and make necessary changes.

Many managers, when faced with this type of employee, take the easy way out—they stop giving corrective feedback.

"Heavens," you think. "Imagine, never getting criticized again. Wouldn't that be wonderful?" But there is a downside to this state—if you never receive negative feedback then it becomes difficult to correct errors and improve.

A bank manager told me one time that when people, in his words, "screwed up," he'd call them into his office, tell them what they did wrong and give them pretty direct feedback on what they had to do to change. If people became defensive, he explained, his method of handling that was to not correct them in the future. "Of course," he continued, quite proud of his people skills, "I would never recommend them for a promotion either. I just tried to ship them off to another branch where I wouldn't have to argue with them all the time."

People who don't improve don't progress in the organization.

Trying to remain non-defensive, especially in the face of personal criticism, is very difficult. We all have a natural tendency to justify ourselves to protect our egos from this unwarranted attack. We begin to explain how it wasn't our fault, how there were extenuating circumstances, how someone else was to blame, how we are not to blame. In other words, our defence shield goes up and the battle is entered into, well and truly.

It is important to separate the criticism of what we do from who we are. Smart people do stupid things from time to time; good people occasionally behave badly and nobody is perfect. Receiving critical feedback about something that you have done does not mean that you are stupid, clumsy, or otherwise incompetent as a person, even if the person giving the criticism is so unskilled as to make that linkage.

TO DO

It is difficult to avoid appearing defensive when you receive criticism. When the criticism is delivered, this is not the time to give reasons why you did what you did (unless you are asked, of course), to blame others for things not going right (even if it was the fault of others), or to complain about how hard, unfair, or unclear the assignment was. A boss who is in the middle of giving you both barrels is unlikely to stop, except to reload, and is unlikely to see those behaviours as being anything but an example of defensiveness in the face of correction.

The first thing you want to say is, "How would you like me to fix it?" Focus on problem solving as opposed to problem analysis. Find out how your boss wants it done, do it that way, and then, when you are calm, and your boss is calm, set up a time to discuss the criticism if you really think that your boss is misjudging you, misinformed, or mistaken.

Focus on what you need to do next time instead on what you should have done last time.

Reduce any possible perception that you are defensive by going in and asking for feedback that will help you improve. Ask for one thing that would make your performance better next time. That way you can control the amount of negative information that might be forthcoming. Say something like, "If there is one thing I could do next time to have a better outcome, what would that be?" Don't say, "Tell me what I need to do in order to improve." This just opens the door to unhelpful dumping.

If you are giving criticism, one way to help reduce defensiveness on the part of the recipient is to begin by asking the person how she might do it differently next time rather than jumping in and accusing her of making a terrible error. People frequently become defensive because it seems to them that their motives are being criticized rather than the outcome. Criticisms that begin with an accusation such as, "If you weren't so lazy you would have had that report in on time," are bound to create a defensive reaction in most people, not because the report is late but because of the personal attack and judgement of their motives.

Begin by suggesting that you believe the person had a good motive for doing what she did. If you are very skilled, you may want to suggest that you understand and approve of the motive if not of the results. For example: "I know you intended to be helpful by cleaning up the files and making it easier for all of us to find what we need. And I appreciate staff taking the initiative to improve things in their area of work. So, I can understand that you may be confused why some people are upset with you this morning. Unfortunately, when you cleared out the files you didn't check with the people who used them as to how they identify current customers and their current files went out with the old files."

Give all criticism in private, not at staff meetings, in hallways, or in other public places. When there is an audience for criticism, people are much more likely to defend their reputation, especially if they think that others in the group should share some of the responsibility for the mistake.

Distinguish between what needs to be corrected and what needs to be ignored. New employees especially are on a steep learning curve and it can be demoralizing to hear nothing but criticism. No one will remain totally non-defensive in the face of unremitting criticism. Start with the one major correction that will make a difference and be sure to balance the criticism with appropriate and sincere recognition of things done right. The appropriate balance should be five positive comments for every corrective comment.

E
IS FOR EFFORT

I don't care how hard you try. If you are in New York and you want to get to Los Angeles and you head east, you're in trouble.

— *Pat Pitsel*

JASON WALKED INTO FRANK'S OFFICE hauling the office whiteboard, laptop and projector, and several large binders.

"Hey, Frank, buddy, I've got that promotional piece you asked me for a while ago. Me and the group have been working on this night and day and you are going to be amazed. Be prepared to be truly blown away by the sheer brilliance of what you are going to see. The group really outdid themselves this time."

He dropped a large binder in front of Frank. The cover boldly declared: "Proposal for Frank Tarnowski, Dispatch Manager for PLP Ltd." In only slightly smaller letters, the words, "Created by Jason Mackay, Manager, Sales and Marketing, PLP Ltd." appeared below. As Frank struggled to rescue his coffee cup, which was in danger of being knocked off his desk, Jason positioned the laptop and whiteboard on the small conference table at the other end of the office.

"Okay, let's see what it looks like," Frank said, trying to remember just how long ago he had originally asked for some help on promotional materials for the new service delivery plan.

As he watched Jason set everything up and begin to show PowerPoint visuals, his eyes widened. As Jason had promised, it truly was spectacular. There was music, animation, video clips, and an endorsement from someone who Frank thought might be the local weatherperson on one of the local TV channels. Frank began to understand why it had taken Jason so long to get back to him with some materials. The problem was that it didn't have anything to do with the service that Frank had to present to the public and their customer base. Perhaps Jason had brought the wrong presentation?

"Uh, Jason," Frank began, "what does this have to do with what I asked you to do for our new Customer delivery service?"

"Don't you like it?" asked Jason in disbelief.

"Well, sure, I think it is pretty, ah, very interesting, and exciting," he added as he saw Jason's face begin to redden. He moved a couple of papers from beneath the binder. "It's just that it is, ah, I mean, it isn't quite what I was expecting. And, it, ah, probably won't work for what we are going to be doing."

Jason snapped the top down on the computer and yanked the power cord out of the wall. "Well, after all the work, effort, and time my crew and I spent on this, I would expect just a little more gratitude and appreciation. We put other people on hold to get this done for your group, you know."

TO THINK ABOUT

A student in one of my management courses handed in their group assignment. "I want you to know," he said proudly, "that our group put in over a hundred man-hours on this project."

"Hmm," I thought to myself, "I shouldn't have put all the slow people in one group." Out loud I told him that marks were given on the quality of the work presented and not the amount of time spent on the project and I was sure that his group produced a solid paper.

Whether it is a university instructor or a manager at work is irrelevant. Both are happy that you try so hard, but you are rewarded by marks or dollars and for results, not for the amount of work you put into a project.

It isn't that trying and effort are not important. From a very young age most of us are told to "try harder." Many people translate that to mean that as long as they put in long hours and lug lots of stuff home to work on at night then they should be rewarded, regardless of the outcome of the effort.

Calculating your value to the organization based on the amount of effort you expend rather than on the results you produce can also have the unfortunate consequence of turning you into a martyr. Martyrs are people with thin lips who sigh a lot and say things like, "Fine, I'll do it!" Martyrs, at least in their own minds, work longer and harder than everyone else, and they are frequently disappointed when no one else seems to value their effort.

People who are afraid they cannot produce superior results, or who do not have a clear idea of what a superior result looks like (sometimes due to the ambiguous nature of the project), will attempt to substitute time, or pages, or weight, or some observable quantity, in place of results.

By putting in long hours, they absolve themselves, again, in their own minds, from any blame or recriminations if the work is not up to the standard that it should be. "You can't blame me," they'll cry indignantly, "look at how much time I spent on this."

Frequently things you like to do, and do well, take much less effort than things that you hate. This should give you some hint that it's not the effort that counts but rather the results you achieve that are important.

TO DO

Ask yourself, what three concrete results have I produced or been responsible for in the last month? If I were going to put down my accomplishments at work on a résumé, what would I write? Which is a stronger statement and more indicative of a person's competencies: "I worked hard on a staffing project" or "I proposed a staffing reallocation plan that was implemented and saved the company $300,000 in overtime costs last quarter."

At the beginning of each month write down one significant work result that you are responsible for. Post this where you can see it every day. When you have completed that task, enter the item in a book or on a file card that you will keep, and use them to prepare for your annual performance appraisal.

Write down one or two things that you have been trying to do but so far have not yet accomplished. After each item, write down all the reasons why you haven't been able to get it done. Take a hard look at all the reasons and identify all the ones over which you have some control. You can re-label these "excuses," if you like, but put a due date by each activity and make a plan to accomplish them within your time estimate.

F
IS FOR FAILURE

*Success is not final, failure is not fatal:
it is the courage to continue that counts.*
— *Winston Churchill*

NORMAN WALKED INTO TOM'S OFFICE. Tom glanced up then put his pen down as he saw the look on Norman's face. It was clear that something had gone badly awry. Tom just hoped that it wasn't a personal tragedy.

He motioned Norman over to his side table and poured him a glass of water. Lowering himself into the chair across from him, Tom enquired as to the nature of the problem.

Norman's eyes began to tear as he explained that he had failed his final accounting course and he would only have one more chance to rewrite and pass it in order to receive his professional accreditation—a necessary requirement in his position. With a determined set of his shoulders and a noticeable swallow, Norman handed him an envelope that contained his letter of resignation. He went on to explain that because the company had paid for all his courses and obviously expected that he would be successful in passing all the exams, the honourable course of action would be to resign now rather than have the company pay any additional fees.

Tom couldn't believe his ears. He didn't need Norman to resign. He needed Norman to continue working and doing the solid job that he had been doing up until this point. And he was, quite honestly, confused about Norman's perception that this was somehow a matter of personal honour. People failed exams all the time. They just buckled down and passed them the next time around. Tom didn't know why Norman had not passed but he did have confidence in Norman's ability to master any accounting subject that he faced. Maybe it was a language problem. Maybe he had problems at home. Tom thought back to his own university days where he had been a solid C student but not without repeating a course or two along the way. This was hardly the end of the world.

TO THINK ABOUT

Many people see failure as moral inadequacy—if you make a mistake, somehow you have transgressed a moral rule or obligation. In an attempt to avoid failure, people will play it safe, follow orders, or policy and procedures even when it is clear in a specific instance that following rules is inappropriate. That way, if failure does occur, it's not their fault.

How one deals with failure is established pretty early in life. Some people come from homes where they returned from school and said something like, "Look, Dad, Mom, I got ninety-two per cent on my math test," the reply would be, "That's good, dear, what happened to the other eight per cent?" This focus on the negative, what hasn't been right and how far away from being perfect the child is, frequently produces a child who grows up to be a perfectionist never satisfied unless the result is completely error-free.

It is far more useful to consider failure as a signal that you have more to learn. It is not an indication that you are stupid and can never learn. It is not an indication that you are evil, or malicious, or hopeless. Failure is simply the coinage you pay for learning something new.

Thomas Edison, when asked how many experiments it took him to invent the light bulb, reportedly replied, "A thousand." When asked if he didn't get discouraged when he had faced so many failures, he said, "I didn't have a thousand failures. I just found nine hundred and ninety-nine things that didn't work."

Some people are lucky that they learned to walk before they learned to think about it. Otherwise, they would have experienced an internal dialogue that went something like this:

"Okay, here I am, eleven months old, and starting to walk. Mostly, I'm falling down. Look at that little two-year-old over there. He is really motoring along. I'll never be able to do that. I'm just going to sit down and wait for the stroller. They can roll me around for the rest of my life."

Fortunately, most of us probably figure that the way you learn to walk is by falling down, and tripping, and stumbling a lot, and that if you get really good at that, then it leads to walking.

There is a foolproof way of never making another mistake—don't try anything new.

When we fail, we usually have one of two responses: either we quit and never try it again, or else we look around for somebody or something to blame it on. In neither case do you learn anything from the failure. If your tendency is to quit as soon as you experience failure, then try to remember the chemist who quit after developing Preparation G.

Failure is destructive when you don't learn anything from it and keep making the same mistake over and over. Ironically, it may be the very fear of failure that creates so much anxiety that people are not capable of learning from their mistakes. If the criticism they receive from failure is severe they don't learn how to do the task correctly the next time. Instead, they concentrate on how to avoid getting caught, on how to avoid doing the task at all, or on how to pass the blame/responsibility off onto someone else so they won't get criticized again. Instead of being able to concentrate on how to learn from their mistake, all their psychic energy is wrapped up in trying to protect their shaky sense of self-esteem.

TO DO

How should you deal with failure if you are the one who has failed? First of all, it's important to try and be as rational as possible about the situation. Don't over-exaggerate the extent of the failure. Oftentimes something fails because of one small component, yet people will react as if the whole endeavour is worthless. Generally, something can be salvaged from a failure, and there are numerous instances of a failure really being an opportunity in disguise. The mould that grew on Alexander Fleming's petri dish ruined the experiment he had been working on but it also led to the discovery of penicillin.

Next, once you have identified the extent of the failure, you need to determine, again as rationally as possible, what your role was in this situation and what you need to do differently next time.

Many people, again due to early learning, seek to look first to an external source or cause for failure, and they end up blaming outside agents for whatever happens. It's the "stupid racquet" syndrome. The player misses the ball and it's the fault of the racquet, an uneven court, the sun was in his eyes, he didn't have breakfast… anything and everything, except that maybe the shot was just too difficult for him to return.

It helps to distinguish between making a mistake and being a failure. Smart people make more mistakes than do stupid people—that's what makes them smart. They make a mistake and learn from it. Stupid people make a mistake and never try again, so they don't learn how to fix or avoid mistakes. They stay stupid.

Remember: "Good judgment is what you get from experience and experience is what you get from bad judgment!"

How do you deal more effectively with the failures of people who work for or with you?

Do you see your role as a coach who has the responsibility of improving the performance of his staff, or do you see your role as a judge whose function it is to pass sentence on those who fail?

If you manage as a "judge," then you create an environment where your staff will put energy into not getting caught and blamed when things go wrong. If you manage as a "coach," then failures are opportunities for learning and staff are free to work at improving their skills and trying new things.

G
IS FOR GAMES

Things are seldom what they seem. Skim milk masquerades as cream.
— *W.S. Gilbert, H.M.S. Pinafore*

LORI GLANCED OUT OF HER office door and saw Amanda hurrying to her desk, lunch bag in hand, coat over her arm, and a guilty look on her face. Late again—the fourth time in two weeks.

Lori sighed. She guessed she'd have to do something about this, and sooner rather than later. She worked hard at being a fair supervisor, trying to be empathic with the problems her various staff members experienced in their personal and professional lives. She could remember too well the previous managers she'd had had who ruled by terror and fear, seemingly caring only that the work get done with no regard for the feelings of the people they managed. Now that she was a manager she would treat her people differently and better. She was responsible for seeing that the work got done. But she was determined that she would be understanding and fair.

She went to her office door and quietly beckoned to Amanda who was starting up her computer. Amanda got up and came quickly over to the open doorway. Lori motioned her in and shut the door behind them both.

"Amanda," she started, "we need to have a talk about lateness."

"Oh, I'm really sorry about this morning," Amanda blurted out, not giving Lori a chance to continue. "I slept in."

Lori motioned her to sit down at the round little side table. "Well, this is not the first time that you have been late. As a matter of fact, this is the fourth time in the past two weeks. Is there a problem I should know about?"

Amanda chewed a fingernail. "I just can't seem to get up in the mornings," she confessed.

"Have you got an alarm clock that you use?"

"Oh yes. I set it every night, but I never seem to hear it in the morning."

"Well, I know about that. I'm a sound sleeper too," Lori smiled, trying to be supportive and understanding. "Have you tried getting one with a louder ring?"

"Oh, I use a clock radio alarm," said Amanda brightly, "I like to wake up to some good ol' foot stompin' country music. Nothing like a good tune to start your day off right."

"Do you turn the volume up loud enough to wake up in the morning?" asked Lori.

"Yes, but it can't be too loud," said Amanda, "because I listen to the same station at night when I go to bed, and if it's too loud I can't get to sleep."

"Have you considered buying a special alarm clock, not just your radio alarm, so that it will have a special sound that you will wake up to? Lori offered.

"I tried that once," said, Amanda, "but it didn't work. I kept turning the alarm off so I could hear the radio and then just went back to sleep."

"How about putting the alarm clock across the room so that you can't just turn it off automatically?" Lori suggested.

"That's a great idea, but then it would be so loud that everyone else in the house would be awake and they would be mad at me for not shutting the noise off right away."

"Perhaps you need a different sound to listen for." Lori was beginning to feel desperate. "Do you have a phone in your room?"

"Sure," answered Amanda, "Doesn't everybody?"

"How about having one of your friends call you and wake you up early enough so that you won't be late?"

"That could probably work," said Amanda slowly, "but I don't think that I would hear the phone either."

"Can you get anyone else in your family to wake you up in the morning?"

"That would be a good idea. My mom use to wake me up when I was in high school." Amanda smiled at the memory. "But now I have to be up so much earlier, and she doesn't get up before me. And everybody else gets up after I do."

Lori wondered, for a brief moment, if any one else in the family got to work on time either. "Could you maybe get to bed earlier the night before so you aren't so tired?" She felt she was getting on to shaky ground here, but viable suggestions were fast disappearing. Still, she maintained a calm and pleasant tone.

"But when I got to bed early I can't fall asleep. I think I'm just not a morning person."

Lori began to understand, in a dim sort of way, why many of her previous managers never seemed to want to help staff with their problems.

TO THINK ABOUT

A number of years ago Eric Berne, the founder of Transactional Analysis, wrote a book called *Games People Play*, and he was not referring to football or baseball. The games Berne referred to were ritualized behaviors that occur over and over as if there were a set of actions that had to be played out again and again, with people playing the same role or set of roles.

He identified games such as "Victim," "Wooden Leg," "Let's You and Him Fight," "Poor Me," "If It Weren't For You," "Yes But," and dozens of others. These kinds of games are played out daily in offices all across the world and consume a phenomenal amount of time and energy. Forget all the time that is supposedly "stolen" by employees who are late to work or take extended coffee and lunch breaks. The time (not to mention the sheer energy) that is lost to productive business because people are engaged in and playing games consumes millions of dollars every year.

TO DO

The first step in combating games is to recognize that they're being played. You have just seen one game in action and if you have a sense that you have "been through his before," chances are you have.

Lori found herself in the not uncommon game of "Yes But." No matter what good suggestion she could offer to Amanda, the response would always be that the suggestion was great, but there was a good reason why it wouldn't work. "Yes But" works so long as one person keeps giving suggestions to the other about how to solve the problem. If you find yourself in the "Yes But" game, an effective corrective technique is to ask the person to come up with a solution that will work for both parties.

Don't take responsibility for other people's problems. Don't you have enough of your own to solve? Besides, the only person who can solve a problem is the person who owns the problem. By making all sorts of suggestions to Amanda about how she might make it to work on time, Lori assumed responsibility for something that is really Amanda's problem to solve. Lori's job as manager is to ensure that Amanda is aware that she is required to be on work on time. Amanda's job is to figure out how to do that.

Refuse to play the game. Of course, you have to recognize that the game is being played in order to refuse to play it. How do you know if there is a game going on or not?

Look for patterns, especially patterns that result in bad feelings rather than problem solving. If the same type of problem keeps happening with a person and no change occurs, then you might be stuck in a game. If, for example, you feel as if you are the dumping ground for everyone's problems and complaints, ask yourself what part you are playing in running the local chapter of Whiners Anonymous.

If someone wants to blame you, dump all over you, or set you up for a blindsided attack, don't participate in the game. Games take two or more to play. Just smile sweetly and say, "Sounds like a personal problem."

It is not always possible to avoid game players, unfortunately, but it is usually possible to avoid the game.

H
IS FOR HUMOUR

Everything is funny as long as it's happening to someone else.
—*Will Rogers*

NORMAN HURRIED DOWN THE CORRIDOR to his office and tried to open the door only to find it partially blocked by a very large cardboard box. The box had "Fragile" stickers, and "Handle With Care" notices pasted all over it and was firmly closed with packing tape.

He looked for a mailing address, but nothing appeared on the top indicating who the recipient was supposed to be or where it had originated. This was puzzling. He wracked his brains. What could he have ordered that would have come in such a big container?

Perhaps the mailing label was on the bottom. He struggled to turn the box over carefully, and heard a loud thump as it went onto its side.

No label on the bottom, either. How did this get to his office and who sent it, he wondered. Leaving the box on its side for a moment, he moved over to his desk and phoned Shipping and Receiving. No one there seemed to know anything about a large package and certainly no one has delivered anything to his office.

Norman regarded the package, lying on its side in front of his desk. Frank's head poked around his door.

"Hey, Norman! Is it your birthday or something?" He grinned.

"No, it's not, "Norman began, turning to face Frank. "Ah, you are making a joke. I'm not expecting any packages, but this has been delivered to my office. Do you think I should open it?" He walked around it warily, fingers tapping nervously on one arm.

Frank's smile broadened. "For sure! If it's in your office it must be for you."

"Maybe you're right." Norman still sounded doubtful as he grabbed a pair of very large scissors from his desk. He began to attack the box that was now on the side.

"Gee, go easy with the scissors, Norman. You might damage whatever is inside."

Suddenly the top of the box was pushed open with a force that sent Norman sprawling, and out of the box crawled Jason. He had a wide, goofy grin on his face.

"Man, Norman, I thought I was a goner there. I thought you were going to stick me like a pig on a spit."

Norman scrambled to his feet, sputtering. His face grew red. "Jason, what are you doing in that box? Who sent you to me? What is going on?"

Frank grabbed Norman's hand, which was still clutching the open scissors. "Whoa, Norman, easy. It's a joke. You've been looking a little stressed lately and we wanted to brighten your day. That's all."

"I don't get it.," said Norman, firmly holding on to the scissors. "How does sending me an anonymous box brighten my day?"

"Well, I guess some people just don't have a sense of humour," muttered Jason as he grabbed the box flaps and began hauling the empty box out of the office.

TO THINK ABOUT

What makes you laugh? What do you find funny?

Everyone agrees that having a sense of humour is one of the most important characteristics that a manager—indeed any individual—can possess. While most people will admit to being deficient in some area, almost no one will admit to not having a sense of humour.

However, there is far from universal agreement on what constitutes the appropriate use of humour in the work place. Jokes that amuse some can annoy others. Actions that reduce some people to uncontrollable laughter may create uncontrolled fury in other folks.

There have been a number of well-publicized instances of people losing their jobs because of the sharing what are deemed inappropriate jokes or videos from the Internet. There is frequently a very large gap between what we may enjoy on a cable TV program and that which would be considered appropriate at the office.

Telling jokes at the office can be high-risk behaviour because there probably is no joke that everyone will find funny. The joke may not offend anyone, but some might find it boring, confusing, unintelligible, predictable, or just plain lame!

Because of all the puzzled looks I received, I stopped telling one of my favourite jokes ("Do you want a beer?" asked the bartender to Descartes. "I think not," Rene said, and disappeared.) Once you have to explain a joke it really isn't funny any more.

Some types of jokes go in and out of fashion. Puns, considered an art form in the time of Shakespeare can today result in people running the other way when they see you coming. Remember elephant jokes? Grape jokes? (Alexander the Grape was one of my favourites.)

Scott Adams, the Dilbert creator, had a wonderful panel where he had the pointy-haired manager musing that experts say that managers should use humour in times of stress such as occurs in periods of downsizing. He goes to a worker and says, "Knock, knock." The employee answers with the usual, "Who's there?" and the manager responds, "not you any more." Is this funny? I guess it would depend on whether or not you were about to lose your job.

Having a sense of humour is not the same thing as being able to tell jokes, repeat funny stories, or walk around smiling constantly, although people who have a sense of humour may often be found doing some of these things.

Humour is a way of seeing the world in a different way, with a different perspective. It involves reframing of what you see or experience. If you put a different frame or matt around a picture it often makes you see that picture in a different way. Your eye notices different things, sees colours in a different way. Reframing, in a psychological sense, involves seeing your environment in a different way by changing the context surrounding the event.

Something that is humorous makes you laugh aloud, chuckle, or merely smile, but nearly always presents you with a perspective that is unexpected. It prevents you from being a victim, from getting over-stressed, and helps you to become more creative.

Let me give you an example.

I make my living talking to groups of people. Some groups are small, some are large. Some groups spend a short time with me, some a long time. Occasionally, there are people who are in those groups who either don't like what I say, or how I say it. And their criticism may be direct, vocal, and immediate, or it may be quieter, indirect (the person with the folded arms, scowl, squinty eyes) and be given later (written comments like "That was trash!").

It doesn't happen often, but it does happen.

The presentation is over. I can't change what I have said or ask the person what the problem is so that I can address the issue, if indeed there is one. So there isn't much point in stewing over that person's reaction. (On the other hand, if 99% of the group reacts that way then I'm not going to reframe the situation. Instead I ask myself what I need to do to improve.)

A sense of humour will help you keep things in perspective and will help you understand that there are few things that can't be repaired, rebuilt, or renewed. Most of all, a person with a sense of humour keeps herself in perspective, not over- or underestimating her importance and significance to a project.

TO DO

Start your own humour file. Collect jokes, cartoons, faxes, and write down funny things that happen to you, to your colleagues, and to your family. When you are stressed, take two or three minutes and read through the file.

Join your company's social club, if there is one, and help to organize fun activities for the staff. Vary these widely so that most people will be able to find something of interest. Not everyone finds paintball fun or golf enjoyable.

Take a humour break every day. Think of something you really had fun doing and relive that experience in your mind for two or three minutes.

Come into work early one morning and leave a cookie, anonymously, on every one's desk, including your own. Watch the reactions and join in on the guessing game of who left the treat.

Start a list of negative phrases that are not allowed in the office. Fine anyone who uses them and put the money toward a charity or toward special treats on the last day of each month. Humour and negativity cannot co-exist side by side.

Set up a humour bulletin board where people are invited to share jokes, cartoons, and the like. Maintain this board faithfully and change it every Friday evening so it is fresh for Monday morning.

Try some new activity every month. Many people don't try new activities because they think they won't be any good at it and will be embarrassed. It's a difficult mind-set to change but it is a significant "ah-ha" moment when you realize that you don't have to be excellent at something in order to have fun! Think of it this way: if you don't do something because you aren't any good at it, how will you ever get good at it?

Keep a log of how frequently you laugh every day, and what makes you laugh.

Ask yourself a critical question: "Do I love my job and have fun at work?" If the answer is that you love your job but don't have any fun, then perhaps you need to look for a different place to do your job. If the answer is that you don't love your job, then it's no wonder you don't have any fun, and perhaps you need to look at changing your job. I believe that this old saying is true: "Do what you love and you will never work another day in your life."

I

IS FOR INDISCRETION

*An indiscreet man is more hurtful than an ill-natured one;
for as the latter will only attack his enemies, and those he wishes ill to,
the other injures indifferently both friends and foes.*

— *Addison*

TOM, LORI, AND JULIA SAT around a table in the crowded bar. It was hard to hear one another with all the late Friday afternoon noise from office workers getting ready for the weekend.

"This," Lori announced to the two others, has been the week from hell."

"Tell me about it," groaned Tom, trying to attract the attention of the server without much success. "Bet my week was worse than your week"

"Well, if we're going to be competitive about it," Julia interjected, "let me get my story in as well. Did you hear what that jerk Jason did to Norman?"

"Oh yeah," sighed Tom. "I certainly heard about it."

"I heard that Jason nearly got his head carved off when Norman ripped into the box," Lori offered.

"I heard that Norman nearly had a heart attack when Jason exploded out of the box," Julia said.

"I suppose that this will be just one more employee relations problem that I'll have to deal with," Lori added.

"One more? You mean there are others?" asked Tom.

The noise volume in the bar had gone up with the arrival of half a dozen of the regular Friday evening crowd. Lori had to shout to make herself heard by the other two. "Yeah, I may have to dismiss Amanda for cause."

"You mean Amanda, that cute little blonde who works in your area? Tom said loudly, also trying to be audible over the music and conversation around them. "What on earth could she have done to warrant dismissal for cause?"

Julia noticed people at the next table looking their way. One of them looked familiar and Julia searched her memory. Then it hit her—it was at the last Christmas party—he was Amanda's date. She flashed him an embarrassed smile, and turned back to her two table companions. "Uh, guys," she said, "do you think we should be talking in public about who we are planning to dismiss?"

TO THINK ABOUT

Being discreet is absolutely critical for a sense of trust to develop between staff and the manager. Managers often become aware of very sensitive issues involving their staff. If any employee ever feels that something told to the manager in confidence was let out, trust will evaporate and make the working relationship very difficult. Once trust has been betrayed it is almost impossible to restore it.

Discretion has two parts: the ability to keep personal information confidential and the maturity to not blurt out the first thing that comes into your mind.

Some people just cannot keep things confidential. Even if it isn't a secret, per se, some people cannot seem to figure out just when they should pass on information, to whom and in what context, and when to keep information private.

The compulsion to share secrets with others is fairly easy to understand—the secret teller becomes the centre of attention. While it is true that most of us hate to be gossiped about, it is equally true that the majority of us just love to listen to gossip about someone else. So the situation is often that the person who is indiscreet usually finds a willing and eager audience, filling that person's need for attention.

Can you tell your spouse/partner the secrets you have learned? It's silly to say no, but your significant other must also understand that she or he is bound by the same rule of discretion and confidentiality that you are. If your partner reveals information you've passed on, then it is the same as if you blabbed it.

Some people can manage not to tell secrets or disclose confidential information but are less adept at avoiding indiscreet remarks. They are the types who will blurt things out, only to see a crimson tide move up the person's neck and face and then recognize belatedly that they have said something that ought best to have been left unsaid. How do you know in advance if something is best not talked about? There are some obvious areas that one should avoid, just on general principle: suicide, divorce, difference in ages with people who are appearing as a couple; asking personal questions about money, sex, religion, politics, weight, bodily functions; and criticizing absent people. The old saying "It is better to keep your mouth shut and be thought a fool than to open it and remove all doubt" is not a bad principle to keep in mind when you are first introduced to a new group of people. Until you have time to listen and discover what the appropriate topics of conversation are, it's better to listen and let the people who are in the know take the conversation lead. Some people's anxiety, and need to be noticed and liked, however, is so great that under sheer nervousness they blurt out the most astonishing things.

You Never Know What You Don't Know

TO DO

Hold discussions about personnel (or personal) matters in enclosed office space. Do not discuss private or confidential matters in elevators, washrooms, hallways, or restaurants or bars.

Be wary about discussing how much you make or your sexual exploits (or lack thereof). Comments on these issues are often perceived as either bragging or complaining. On the flip side of this, do not ask personal questions about money, sex, religion, politics, weight or bodily functions. Don't criticize or tell embarrassing stories about absent colleagues. These stories always get back to the person.

Don't promise in advance to keep a secret—the "If I tell you something will you promise not to tell anybody?" query. Tell the person that you can't promise until you know what is being asked.

Sports teams have an interesting practice. They teach their players that "what goes on in the team locker room stays in the locker room." This is a useful credo for employees. Don't tell people outside of your office about the problems inside your office. If these problems are severe enough to talk about, then the comments should be directed at the person best in position to do something about it.

If your job makes you privy to confidential information about staff or clients, never divulge that information outside of official, job-related channels. Just because you work in payroll, for example, doesn't mean that you can tell others, inside or outside of the company, what anybody earns.

J

IS FOR JUDGMENT

Good judgment comes from experience.
Experience comes from bad judgment.
— *Anonymous*

FRANK READ THE MEMO FROM Karim over, and then over again, and then reached for the phone. He couldn't believe that Karim, their IT Manager, was going to install a major update on everybody's computer over the weekend without any conversation with the rest of the team. This was going to create a major headache for everyone except those who worked with computers for a living. He could just imagine the reaction he would get from all his people when they came in on Monday morning and found that things did not look the same as they did when they left on Friday. And there really was no point in talking to Karim about this because he obviously did not understand anybody who couldn't use his programs. He was just going to have to be firm and let Karim know that approaching a software change in this manner was a huge error in judgement. He obviously didn't understand the staff and their needs.

Karim was both puzzled and angry after he finished the phone call from Frank. He and his team had been working practically non-stop to ensure that the transition to the new program was going to be practically seamless. The new program would use the same commands as the old one did but it has some additional features that would make everyone's job much easier. Of course it looked different in order to highlight the new features, but people were smart enough to be able to figure that out, surely.

As he reflected on Frank's comments, most of which he thought grossly unfair, his temper began to rise. For the past three months his IT team had had nothing but complaints from Frank's group. Several of Frank's staff had asked for the problems to be fixed but to fix it in a way that meant no downtime for them. He had been positive that everyone would be thrilled that the new software would be up and running for them when they arrived at their desks on Monday morning. This approach had always worked fine at the last company he had worked for.

And now, just when he had a fix, a better program that would solve all the complaints, he gets an angry tirade from a senior manager. How could he have misjudged the reaction of this manager so badly?

TO THINK ABOUT

Like common sense, judgment seems be one of those things that you are mysteriously just born with. How often have you seen someone do something really impulsive and stupid, such as drinking too much at a staff party and telling off the boss, or showing up to work in a see-through top exposing a bare midriff, complete with naval piercing, leaving you to ask yourself, "What on earth were they thinking?"

Good judgment has two parts. One part tells you what you should not do, and the other part tells you what you should do. People who are overly cautious are said to never make the same mistake once. They only focus on the part of judgment that tells them what to avoid.

But judgment is not just caution, nor is it just avoiding action. Good judgment should also tell us how far to go, when to move, when to take the leap.

Someone once said that judgment consists of determining what is wrong while evaluation consists of finding the value in something. Perhaps that's why judgment is often associated with caution and apparent negativity. People who show only that half of good judgment usually manage to avoid errors but they may not necessarily find better ways of doing things.

It is easy to misjudge events, situations, or people when you act in isolation without checking with those outside your own small sphere of operation.

Is good judgment merely a matter of doing what everyone else is doing and avoiding what most others avoid? Some people have become successful by going against the common good judgment of their times and doing what others would not dream or dare to do. We read and hear about successful contrarians. Good judgment, however, should not be confused with good luck or good timing.

Judgment is really not much more than taking time to look at the consequences, evaluate possible outcomes, and select the course of action that promises to be the one that will provide the greatest rate of return. Judgment is the triumph of thinking over feeling. But this is a very cognitive approach to life, and life, for many, is emotional rather than rational.

TO DO

As a manager, how do you develop good judgment in your staff?

One obvious way is to let your people make decisions and accept the consequences for those decisions. If they never have to be responsible for anything, then it's difficult to develop a good judgment about what will and what won't work.

The second step is to conduct a "post-mortem" on all decisions, good and bad, not with an eye to blaming when things do not turn out, but with an eye toward determining what worked and what may need to be done better next time.

Third, when you make decisions, share your reasoning with your staff. "Because I felt like it" obviously won't cut it, so it may mean that you will be forced to tighten up your own decision making ability and enhance your powers of judgment in order to teach your staff.

And finally, don't cut people's hands off at the wrist when they make an error in judgment. Analyze what went on to see where the error occurred. Did she lack information? Training? Is she merely impetuous and acts before getting all relevant information? Sometimes poor judgment is passed off as a character fault or a personality variable—you either have it or you don't. If you believe the latter, then you will never have employees with twenty years of experience; all you will have is employees with one year of experience twenty times!

And if you are not a manager? How do you develop and demonstrate good judgment?

The first thing to do is to consult with others before you do something that you have never done before.

Ask others in your organization how they knew when to take a risk and when to pull back.

Ask yourself what the consequences will be if what you are planning to do is unsuccessful. While no one can control all the variables in a situation, have a back-up plan if something unexpected does occur.

K

IS FOR KUDOS

There is no verbal vitamin more potent than praise.
— Frederick B. Harris

LORI STUCK HER HEAD INTO Norman's office and cleared her throat to attract his attention. "Ah, Norman," she said as he lifted his head, "Can I talk to you a minute or is this not a good time?"

"Certainly, Lori. Please come in," Norman answered as he stood up. "What can I do for you today?" He smiled nervously at her. He did not think that having the HR Manager come to his office was a good sign.

Lori closed the door and moved over to the corner table and took a chair. "Norman, I know this is the first management job you have held with this company, and you've been here six months now. I thought I'd just stop by and see how things were going for you."

Norman looked at her, his face expressionless. "Things are going fine as far as the work goes," he said slowly. He moved around his desk slowly toward the table, picking up a pad of paper from his desk.

"Well, that's good," said Lori. "I know the new reporting and financial system that you have introduced to the team has been very helpful. It gives us a lot more information than we had previously and should help us to stay more focused on our financial goals." She stopped for a moment. Norman's face remained impassive.

"Please, Norman, do sit down. I did want to chat with you about a potential problem that I think we can nip in the bud." Norman put the date on the top page of his pad of paper, and waited, pen in hand, for Lori to continue.

"You know that as head of Human Resources I do get some staff members who come to me for advice, sometimes even before they go to their own manager. I guess they see me as a kind of sounding board. Generally I try to help them think through their problem and work out a way they can talk to their manager about it and come to a mutually agreeable solution.

"I did have a couple of people in my office the other day from your area Norman. They were unwilling to come to you directly and asked if I could speak with you. It seems as if they feel that you don't appreciate their work and that you are very quick to criticize them in public for every little mistake they make. I know that this new reporting system has been challenging to you and the group and that not everything has gone perfectly from the beginning…."

"They should not have come to you, Lori," interrupted Norman stiffly. "If you tell me who they are I will speak to them and ask them why they did not come to me with their concerns."

"Oh, no, Norman, that's not why I am here. I came because I wanted to suggest that you might be able to balance some praise with the criticism that you feel is necessary. The conversion to our new system has been very complex and I'm sure that not everything went exactly the way you wanted it to the first time. Your group has worked very hard and put in long hours to get it up and running. They must have done some things right in order for us to get the reports we are now receiving. How do you think they feel when they hear about their mistakes but don't hear anything about the successes?"

"They should know when they are doing it right because I don't criticize them," replied Norman logically. "They are not babies that I have to praise every time they do their job."

Lori sighed to herself. This was going to take longer than she had planned.

TO THINK ABOUT

Kudos are bits of acknowledgement that you give others when they have done something noticeable. Kudos are public and draw attention to the good works that have been performed. Too often when someone has accomplished something of note, other people in the office ignore it, or even worse, appear to be jealous of it. They will discount the achievement by suggesting that the person must have "brown-nosed" in order to have accomplished it, was the recipient of blind luck, or that they paid somebody off in order to have been successful.

It demonstrates a generosity of spirit and a sense of being secure with oneself to acknowledge the good things that other people have done.

When you acknowledge other people's accomplishments, particularly if the others are peers, it builds alliances because you are then in the position of an ally rather than a competitor.

An acknowledgment of other people's accomplishments is also one very productive way of handling those people who are continually boasting and bragging about everything they do. It can indeed be very tiresome to constantly have to connect with people who are always boasting about their accomplishments, but then, perhaps the reason they feel they have to boast is because no one else ever acknowledges that they do anything.

If you can hand out kudos before the other person has to ask for them, you help the other person feel that s/he exists, help yourself to be more in control of the conversation, and you get a reputation of being a generous soul. Not bad for a simple acknowledgement of something a person has done well.

TO DO

Praise in public, criticize in private is a good rule to follow.

Hand out kudos before people ask for them.

Acknowledgment is food for the soul. Kind people who would never deny a starving person food can be downright malicious in denying people acknowledgement, which is every bit as great a need as is food. Without acknowledgement a human's psychic survival is in doubt. Be the first in your group to tell what others have done right. Be the last to spread around what they have done wrong.

Keep a list of the kudos you hand out and for whom. If you have people in your group who haven't received kudos from you in over four weeks, then you need to spend more time looking for something positive.

Do you think that you are already pretty good at handling out deserved compliments? Take the five-cent test. Put five pennies in a pocket. Every time you give kudos to someone for something they have done well, transfer one penny to another pocket. When you have transferred all five pennies, then, and only then, can you administer one correction or give a critical comment.

L
IS FOR LANGUAGE

*Some guy hit my fender and I said, 'be fruitful and multiply,'
but not in those words.*
— *Woody Allen*

"NOW, JUST CALM DOWN, SWEETIE," said Frank with his hands waving in front of him.

"Don't you 'sweetie' me," snarled Julia, her voice rising both in pitch and volume. "I've had enough of your male chauvinistic bullshit, and I'm not going to stand for it any more."

"Hey," he replied, backing up toward her desk. "Don't blame me. If you can't run with the big dogs, then don't get off the porch. Or maybe you'd prefer the girl's version," he added sarcastically. "If you can't stand the heat, stay out of the kitchen."

"Why you misogynistic son of a b..." began Julia when the tall figure of Tom filled the doorway.

"You two are putting on quite the show for the rest of the office," he said. "I, and everyone else on this floor, can hear you two all the way down the hall. Frank, in my office now, please."

Frank turned and stalked out.

Tom turned to Julia, "Frankly, I'm surprised. I didn't expect to hear that kind of language from one of my senior managers, let alone a woman. I'm going to talk to Frank and calm him down, and then I expect that you will offer him an apology." Tom followed Frank out of the office leaving Julia scarcely able to believe her ears.

TO THINK ABOUT

Watch your language. There really isn't a subtle way to get this point across. This means not only no type of profanity, but also no derogatory terms about women, men, minorities, or people of other cultures and beliefs.

Is there a double standard at work here? In terms of profanity, sure! Men can often "get away" with vulgar language, especially in all-male groups, in ways that women cannot. But it's risky for both. Large constituencies of people object to certain kinds of language, including such "mild" expression as "oh hell," or "damn."

Back in the early seventies I did a master's degree at Fordham University in New York City. As part of the program I did a counselling practicum at an experimental high school in downtown Manhattan. The profanity used by students toward one another, and toward the faculty, astounded me, coming as I did from a small city on the Canadian Prairies. It seemed that the F-word was used as every part of speech in a sentence—verb, noun, adjective, adverb, interjection, gerund, participle—everything except a pronoun. It was when I heard it inserted in the middle of another word (I believe it was fanf&^&ingtastic!) that I realized that it truly was no longer taboo. Not only was it not taboo, it was not always used as a sign of intense anger (unless, of course, it had the word "mother" attached to it in some way).

So we have a major disconnect between generations. Very few people under thirty, both male and female, have not used that famous word while very few women over fifty-five have ever said it out loud at work.

Men and women have always used words differently, and probably always will. Studies show that, in general, women use less slang, speak more formally in conversations, and are more likely to use grammatically correct sentences. But there are fewer and fewer opportunities for the sexes to work in single-sex groups and the differences in how the two sexes use language can create tension and stress in the workplace.

Men get stressed because they feel they constantly have to self-monitor the words they speak for fear of offending some woman in their group. Women, especially if they constitute a small minority of females in a male group, feel pressure to adopt the male language habits. They may feel that they have to use profanity to show that they fit in and are just "one of the gang."

The double standard may be alive and well in your workplace, but there is no double standard when it comes to using derogatory terms referring to other racial or religious groups. Neither gender should engage in male or female bashing, sexist rhetoric, or language that expresses contempt for others. Some people may label this as being the obsession of some anal-retentive language cop or super-sensitive wimp. But it is a validation of the idea that words do have power to hurt or to heal. Remember the old saying, "Sticks and stone may break my bones but words will never hurt me?" If words did not have the power to hurt we would not have had to learn that verse.

It is not just profanity that we need to watch out for, however. Men often define bravery and courage in terms of their anatomy, which can create some problems in trying to describe courageous women. "She really has balls" is seen by some men to be a compliment in much the same way "she thinks like a man" is seen as a positive observation. Most women perceive the first as silly, not to mention anatomically incorrect, and the second as dismissive, implying that men's thinking is superior to that of women's thinking.

TO DO

Ask a friend to monitor your language and let you know if you're overusing profanity or some other speech or language mannerisms that are not professional.

Wear an elastic band around your wrist. Every time you use profanity, snap it to remind yourself to use other terms.

Be careful about using profanity to "fit in" —doubly so if you are female. Women frequently think that they have to cuss like a guy in order to be accepted by the guys. Men do not think that women who swear are just "one of the guys." They think they are women with a dirty mouth.

There is no excuse for using derogatory racial terms, even under the guise that the recipient doesn't mind it. And if you are a member of a visible minority subjected to racial slurs, just smile and say, "How 18th century of you to notice!" Words used to shock or hurt cease to be useful weapons when they appear to have no impact. I am reminded of the cartoon of a woman sitting at her desk with a large sign in front, reading "Sexual harassment that occurs at this desk will not be reported, it will be graded."

If you are in a position of authority, however, you cannot allow disrespectful or objectionable language to occur without censure. To remain silent gives tacit approval to behaviour that should not be tolerated by organizations.

M
IS FOR MOODY

We boil at different degrees.
— *Ralph Waldo Emerson*

JASON SLIPPED INTO TOM'S OUTER office. "Rebecca," he asked, 'what kind of mood is Tom in today?"

"I haven't seen him yet this morning, Jason. Why do you ask?"

"I have to give him some bad news about our sales figures and if he's in one of his 'moods,'" Jason made air quotes with his fingers, "then I sure don't want to be the one to bring him the bad news—not until his mood improves, any way."

"Oh, so if he's in a good mood, you want to put him in a rotten mood so the rest of us suffer, is that it?" laughed Rebecca.

"Well, no, that's not what I mean. But you know how difficult he can get sometimes, and I'm never sure just what sets him off. Maybe I can just leave him a voice message and tell him I'm out of town for the rest of this week. Would that work, do you think?"

"Tell you what, Jason, suppose I phone you when he comes in and give you a heads up?"

"You're the best, Rebecca. Although I'll be worrying all morning until I know whether I can go and see him today or decide to put it off. How can you work for somebody like that?"

TO THINK ABOUT

A problem that many managers and staff have to deal with in the work environment is the moody employee. Staff who cannot predict the mood of their boss, except to know that it won't be the same from one day—or even from one event to the next—spend a lot of time in unproductive strategizing. Instead of working they are trying to figure out the best way to get what they need. In some studies it has been shown that staff would rather have a consistently difficult person to work with rather than someone who was always up and down, because at least with the former you could try to develop a strategy that might work.

Managers who have moody employees never know when to approach them, are wary of providing corrective feedback, and spend a lot of time listening to other employees who have trouble dealing with the moody one.

Moody behaviour on the part of the boss exacerbates co-dependent behaviour on the part of employees. Instead of worrying about the quality of their work, they worry about the mood of the boss. They are constantly looking for how and when to approach the boss. Plans are made not on the value of the result, but on whether or not they can be sold to a person, depending on the mood he is in. Employees become very strategic with moody bosses.

This is not just a female issue, although women do seem to form a larger group of employees who are seen to be moody. (A female comedian commented that it wasn't fair: women got PMS and men got ESPN.)

Many people have no idea why they are in a good or bad mood. These people just seem to wake up in one of their moods. Others have their moods "thrust upon them" by external forces. They may begin the day in a good mood, but some external event—a flat tire, a fight with their significant other, rain when they wanted it to be sunny—can put them in a bad mood. Both of these types of people tend to avoid responsibility for their mood shifts, attributing them to something outside their control. It could be PMS, low blood sugar, a migraine, or whatever the disease of the decade seems to be. Whatever it is, they see themselves as victims, unable to control their emotions and moods.

TO DO

What can—or should—you do if you are just a moody person? Although moodiness is not the same as bi-polar mood disorder (manic-depressive illness), personal counselling can be of benefit. People who are constantly moving from highs to lows are difficult to deal with as co-workers; as managers or employers, they are almost impossible. They may not be crazy, but they tend to drive everyone else around them crazy.

Check with an office mate who will be honest with you and ask if s/he or others in the office would consider you moody. If you get a "yes," don't let that answer send you off into one of your moods. As difficult as it might be, thank the person for the honest response, and then book an appointment with your doctor. Sometimes moods can be due to physical causes. If the checkup clears you of anything physically wrong, then seriously consider professional counselling.

If you have a boss who is moody, start looking for another place to work or develop a thicker skin. Bosses almost never change unless the staff is able to go over his/her head and talk to the next level of management.

If possible, talk with the next level of management, but be aware that this may backfire and you may have to start looking for a new job.

N
IS FOR NEGOTIATE

*You cannot negotiate with someone who says,
'What is mine is mine, and what is yours is negotiable.'*
— John F. Kennedy

JASON STOPPED BY NORMAN'S OFFICE and squeezed his way in past three boxes, two chairs, and four filing cabinets.

"Man, Norman, you are really squeezed in here. I don't see how you can possibly find anything. And I thought my office was messy." He laughed as a pile of papers toppled off the chair he was moving.

'Yes, you are right, Jason," said Norman, moving sideways to retrieve the papers. "Please sit down." He shifted the pile of papers on top of a stack of books on his desk.

"Why don't you ask for a bigger office?" asked Jason. "With all the work that you have to do and the files you are responsible for, I don't see how you can possibly be expected to keep everything straight in this broom closet."

"I'm sure that if Tom thought I should have a bigger office he would assign one to me," replied Norman somewhat defensively.

"Norman, the squeaky wheel gets the grease." He paused as he saw Norman frowning.

'I'm not sure I understand what a squeaky wheel has to do with my office," Norman said, his brows still drawn tightly together in consternation.

'It's just a saying, Norman," Jason explained. "My mom used it all the time. Don't you have a saying like that in your country?" He waited to see if this helped to clear Norman's apparent confusion.

"This is my country, Jason," Norman answered softly,

Jason's face reddened. "Oh well, yeah. Sure. Of course. I mean…." His voice trailed off. Norman said nothing but continued to look at Jason. Shaking his head, Jason continued hurriedly.

"What I meant was, "If you don't ask, you don't get! If you don't ask, the answer is always 'no.' What else can I tell you? How do you think I got that big corner office? Anyway, I just stopped by to drop off those figures you asked for, but I better hand them to you or else you'll never find them again." He gave a small laugh as he handed the file to Norman, squeezed out between the chair and the boxes, and waved goodbye making his way down the hall to his own corner office.

Norman watched Jason's back. Jason was right. He did have the biggest office. And it was a corner office. And he was the newest person on the Management Team.

TO THINK ABOUT

The key principle is that everything is negotiable. Relationships are negotiable, job duties are negotiable, salaries and benefits are certainly negotiable. Just because someone tells you "this is the rule" does not mean that it has never been broken or bent for someone along the line. There are always extenuating circumstances and there are always reasons why things can—and will—change.

The trick is to learn how to ask. Sometimes we don't think that we can negotiate with a person because there is too great a power difference. Both sides must possess something that is desired by the other and be able to deliver it. What is desired might be material or it might be emotional or psychological.

If you can't ask for what you want, it doesn't mean you don't want it. It just means that you may become more devious, complex, manipulative, or cunning about how you go about getting it.

Negotiations still occur, but they do so on a very subtle level. What happens when someone gets angry with you? Have you ever got the cold shoulder? Are you then in the middle of a negotiation? You bet—but it's probable that neither of you call it, nor think of it, as that.

Relationships would be much easier to deal with if these hidden negotiations were brought out in the open and the unmet needs were expressed. The balance of rights and responsibilities always involves a process of negotiation, but sometimes the process becomes derailed when people think they are negotiating about things rather than about more abstract issues.

Generally speaking, we negotiate for things in order to meet personal needs. Many of our most powerful needs are psychological as opposed to physical.

TO DO

What do you do when someone declares that something is "non-negotiable?" First of all, ask yourself what it is that you really want? Perhaps you are hoping for something like respect when you ask for new job title. It is, however, considerably easier to get a new title than it is to get more respect.

What do you have to negotiate with, to exchange, for what you want? If you get more respect, more status, more responsibility, what is your side of the bargain? Many people go in and ask for something. That is not negotiating. That is asking or begging.

Before you begin the negotiating process, decide how important this item is to you both in the short and in the long term.

What is the cost of staying in the relationship, work or personal, with someone who declares that something is non-negotiable?

Second, decide what it is you have to negotiate to exchange for what you want. If you get more respect, what is your side of the bargain?

And finally, before you begin the negotiating process, consider what acceptable options are available to you should you not get what you are negotiating about.

O
IS FOR OFFICE

A clean desk is the sign of a sick mind.
— *office graffiti*

"WAY TO GO, NORMAN. YOU da man!" cheered Jason as he bounded into Norman's new office. Norman, busily unpacking a large carton, looked puzzled.

"I told you to ask for a larger office and you'd get one," said Jason. "This is sweet. I brought you a new office gift. When are you going to have your official open office party?" Jason took a small stuffed voodoo doll wearing a small sign that said "The Boss" from behind his back. "You can put this by your computer and when Tom gets on your nerves you can stick him with one of your wall tacks. Or better yet, staple it to your next report!" Jason howled. "Seriously, man, you'll have to decorate this office now that you can see the walls."

"Oh Jason," Norman said, not reaching for the doll that Jason held out. "I couldn't put that figure on my desk. It would not be respectful. But thank you anyway for thinking of me," he said hurriedly as Jason's grin disappeared. Norman took the doll and placed it gingerly on his desk. "You gave me very good advice about asking for a larger office, and, as you can see," I have been successful."

"Anyway," Jason's good humour returned quickly. "I'm here to give you some professional decorating advice. After all, my office is the talk of the company."

Norman nodded his head. 'That is so true, Jason. Your office is indeed the talk of the organization." He wanted to add that it looked like the dorm room of a college freshman, but he didn't want to hurt Jason's feelings. Instead he tried another approach. "Jason, I think I would like my office to look much like Tom's."

"Like Tom's? " Jason said incredulously. "You must be kidding, Norm. Tom's office is so, so...." Jason struggled for a word.

"Tidy?" asked Norman.

"I was going to say boring," answered Jason. "There is absolutely nothing interesting in Tom's office, except Tom," he added hastily seeing the expression on Norman's face.

"Boring?" said Norman.

"Yeah. No pizzazz. Everything is so neat, so tidy, so, so, so straight. He has the obligatory picture of his wife and kids on the desk, the statement of corporate values on one wall, and his twenty-five-year service award on another. This is all so booorrring!"

"Perhaps," said Norman gently, moving the voodoo doll into his top drawer, "you might want to check the offices of the other managers, Jason."

TO THINK ABOUT

In North America, the size, location and decor of the office you have (or indeed even the lack of an office) is a clear indicator of the amount of status you have in the organization.

Who you are, organizationally speaking, can often be determined by the quality of the carpet, whether you have prints, originals (or any) art on the wall, and whether the desk is made of oak or plywood. There is even a term that derives its existence from these small, but meaningful symbols.

"Rug-ranked" is a term that refers to secretaries (or, as they are now referred to, Administrative Assistants) who move up the organization along with their boss. They are still doing the same job, only now they may be a secretary to a vice-president instead of secretary to a general manager. "Rug-ranked" refers to the ranking or status in the organization based on the quality of the broadloom in the office—the higher the rank of your boss, the better the quality of the carpet, and the higher status (and power) in the organization.

Some organizations, especially government offices, have very clear guidelines about the amount and type of space that employees get based on their job level in the organization. Whether you can have a corner office depends on your position, not on the kind of work you do. In the world of office hierarchy and politics, the corner office (with more windows) denotes a higher status and more power. If you don't have a workspace that reflects your position in the organization, it can send a signal to others that although you have the title you don't really have much power or influence. It may seem silly but it helps to remember that in male-directed and dominated organizations, symbols are signs of status, which in turn are signs of power, and men have very sensitive antennae with respect to power and position.

It's hard to believe that some people do not understand that "big office equals big cheese," so to speak, but that would seem the case when people accept an office or work space that is much smaller than what their colleagues at a comparable level enjoy.

Office space or the lack of it is not the only aspect of your work environment that sends a message to others. How you decorate your office and how you manage the space also reveals much about you, and not always in the ways that you might think. Clutter, files, and paper on top of every available horizontal surface? That says "disorganized" rather than "busy." Multiple pictures of kids and partner, kids' artwork and school projects say "more focused on family than on the company." A bulletin board full of sardonic or satirical cartoons such as Dilbert, or Doonesbury, says "cynic, not a team player" rather than "a person with a great sense of humour works here." Unless you work in a creative agency such as an advertising firm, having an office filled with gag items, stuffed toys, and twenty-five framed photos of you at charity golf tournaments does not send a message of competence or focus.

TO DO

How you decorate and maintain your office or your cube sends some very clear messages to people. If you want to be taken seriously then your office and desk should reflect a level of organization or neatness.

Take a look at the office space of those one level above you in the organization, especially those who are seen as having the potential to rise in the company. What types of personal items are on display in their office? Do they post certificates and diplomas? Do they bring in their own art of pieces of sculpture? Does their office look like an extension of their family room at home, or does it look like a corporate office?

The personal, additional touches that you bring into the office reveal much about you. In most companies having family pictures is pretty standard. People who have a drawing by their kid—you know, the type that says, "Daddy I love you," in three colours and four letter sizes—suggests that you are a caring parent, unless, of course, your child did this when he was four and he is now sixteen. In that case it says that you get stuck in the past and have a hard time moving into the future.

How you arrange your office furniture, given that you have some freedom in this matter, also says much about your approachability and willingness to communicate with others. Talking to others from behind your desk suggests an air of authoritarianism, an "I'm in charge here and don't forget it." Sitting with your face to the wall and back to the door (which is very uncomfortable for most North Americans) conveys a distinct air of "don't approach me."

Have a conversation area (if the space permits) around a coffee table, or a round table away from the desk. This suggests an air of approachability, of "let's discuss this." It also helps you to focus on your visitor and not on your computer screen.

Some people have pictures of themselves with famous people all over their walls. This lets you know that the person is impressed with status and expects you to be impressed with his status. You may be dealing with a person who values style rather than substance.

Needless to say, in this day and age people should refrain from posting materials that others may find offensive—this includes calendars with nudes (either sex), "homey" little sayings of the type that use to be embroidered and hung on the kitchen wall beside the stove, or Xeroxed copies of cartoons that are obviously attempting to humiliate some group or sector of society.

P
IS FOR POLITICS

Those who are too smart to engage in politics are punished by being governed by those who are dumber.
— Plato

LORI PICKED UP THE PHONE slowly. This was not going to be an easy conversation, she knew.

"O'Brien here." The voice was abrupt and dismissive.

"Frank, this is Lori. How are you this morning?"

"I'm fine, but very busy, Lori. What can I do for you?"

She bit back the retort that would have suggested that everybody in the company was busy and that if she were going to make a social call then Frank O'Brien would be the last one on her list to phone.

"Frank, I was wondering about the decision you've made to offer the promotion to Charlie Francis. I've got your paperwork here and I see that you want this to be effective as of last Monday."

"Is there a problem with that?" asked Frank abruptly.

"Actually, there are several problems that we need to talk about, Frank. You know, according to HR policy in the company, no offer or decision should be made regarding new hires or promotions until everything has come through my office. It's important that we ensure that all HR policies are adhered to and that our compensation policy is maintained. I see by your offer letter to Charlie that you are offering him a salary that is above what the position normally gets. But more to the point, Frank, I'm concerned about your offering the promotion to Charlie in the first place."

"Are you trying to tell me that HR can tell me who to promote or not promote? If you want to do my job why don't you just move into my office?"

"Frank, it's not my intent to do your job. But it is my job to make sure that the HR policies in the company are followed by all the managers, including you. My concern with your promoting Charlie is that, on the face of it, Charlie seems much less qualified to do the job than at least three other people in your department. I know you and he play golf together and go to the same church. I am concerned that the people in your department will get the idea that Charlie's promotion is due to some sort of personal favouritism. I'm sure that's not the case and I want to keep any rumours about personal politics from starting in the first place. When can we get together to discuss this?"

TO THINK ABOUT

People often complain about their job because of the politics that are involved. "I really like what I do," they'll say, "It's just all the politics that I hate." (This view obviously does not hold politicians or the profession of politics in very high regard.)

By this, they mean, presumably, that people cannot be straightforward and honest in their dealings with others, that people are likely to say one thing to your face and another behind your back, that little subgroups plot to overthrow those in power, and that people are recognized and promoted because of their relationships rather than on their ability to do good work.

Well of course! Who, in their right mind, would promote an enemy—someone who hates you and is out to cause you injury?

Of course a boss would promote someone he likes or overlook one whom he dislikes. But, you cry, what about ability?

If you are in a highly political type of organization where personal favouritism rather than ability is the sole criteria for recognition and advancement, then one of the sanest approaches is to get out. People who stay in sick or crazy organizations get sick, go crazy. This kind of environment is as poisonous as any toxic emission.

There is another side to politics, however, that merits a closer view. The political process is one that allows us an alternative to grouping together and shooting one another. It is a process that promotes compromise, that attempts to acknowledge just rights of various parties, and that helps you reach workable solutions. Politics does not, in and of itself, have to be duplicitous, insincere, or self-serving.

Politics in an organization can take many forms. It can take the very negative form where there are self-serving groups who seek to get their own way by immoral and/or illegal means, or it can be a pragmatic approach to doing business in an environment where different people have different interests, needs, concerns, and goals.

People who blame politics in the organization for their unhappiness often refer to a perception that jobs do not appear to be given to the deserving, but rather to people who get along with the boss.

The fact is that there is not a lot of difference in ability between many people and perhaps the ability to get along may be more important than the ability to perform some technical function. The difference in ability between people accounts less for productivity than do many more intangible factors such as judgement, ability to elicit cooperation from co-workers, or the ability to determine priorities.

Politics are the rules that govern how the work is done in companies, much the same way that the rules of the game govern how a sport is played. Your choice is not whether or not to engage in playing politics; your job is to decide whether you can live with the type of politics that exist.

TO DO

Destructive political manoeuvring usually exists where there are poor conflict resolution skills. When you have a disagreement or conflict with someone, do you talk to the person involved or to everybody else? If it is the latter, then you are playing politics.

Every organization has some sort of political gamesmanship going on. It's more career enhancing to understand the game than it is to refuse to play the game. Whom do you know in your organization who has some insight into the political games that occur there? Have lunch with that person and check out your perceptions.

Hard to believe though it may be, losing a promotion to another candidate may not be a matter of politics. It may be that you are lacking some critical skill that is necessary to be successful in the job. Rather than blaming politics for your lack of success, follow up and talk to the manager about what you can do to be better positioned to get the promotion next time one comes up.

Play politics in a positive sense by refusing to criticize your boss, the organization, or your co-workers to outsiders or to others in the company.

Q
IS FOR QUALIFICATIONS

Natural ability without education has more often raised a man to glory and virtue than education without natural ability.
— *Cicero*

"THANK YOU FOR COMING IN, Charlie," Lori said, offering her hand and pointing to a chair. "I wanted to talk with you today about the promotional opportunity that recently came up in Frank's area and how we might help you to prepare for the next opening that comes available."

"I should have had that one," said Charlie truculently. "I know how to do that job, and Frank as much as said I was the guy he wanted in that job. Besides, I've been here for ten years now." He sat in the chair, his arms folded, a scowl on his middle-aged face.

'I know that, Charlie," said Lori calmly, "and we want you to be with us for a number of years to come. I also would like you to be fully qualified to apply for the next promotion that opens up. I see by your file here that when you started with us you had a grade twelve certificate and since that time it doesn't appear that you have taken any additional training or courses."

'I didn't have to," interrupted Charlie, leaning forward. "I learned on the job. And I do a good job. Frank and everybody say so. I'm probably better at dispatching than any other guy on any other shift or location."

"You're right," replied Lori. "Your performance appraisals have all been very positive. But I have noticed one pattern, Charlie. Often I see that a course has been recommended as part of the personal development section, but it doesn't appear that you have followed that suggestion. Any particular reason why?"

"This job ain't about book learning. No course or book is going to teach you how to be a good dispatcher. It's something that you just have to learn by doing the job, making mistakes and then not making them any more."

"I understand that, Charlie," Lori said. "But the promotion you had your name in for was a supervisory position, one that requires a different set of skills than the ones you have developed on the job. We don't believe that supervisors should be trained on the job. We want people who have learned something about supervising and dealing with people before they reach the position. That's why we have an employee education plan as part of our benefit package."

"Well, I'm too old to go back to school. If I did go back, not saying that I would, mind you, it would take me five years, and by then I'd be forty."

"How old will you be in five years," Lori asked him, "if you don't go back to school?"

Charlie looked at her quizzically. "Forty," he replied.

"Well then," Lori said, "What else are you going to do while you're hanging around waiting to be forty?"

TO THINK ABOUT

There is no doubt that today the push is on toward acquiring academic credentials. For recent high school graduates the outlook is bleak indeed if they do not possess some sort of post-secondary training. Many workers are caught in a situation where they might have been doing a satisfactory job for a number of years but are prevented from advancing in their careers, or even from transferring to another organization that requires a degree or a certificate for any new hire.

A number of years ago I was asked to fill in for a university instructor who was teaching a communication class in the Faculty of Continuing Education but was unable to teach that particular seminar. I did, and was offered the job of continuing to teach that class in the future. When I enquired what had happened to my predecessor, I was told that it appeared that he did not have either the MA, or the PhD from Harvard that he claimed to have earned.

The paradox was that while he was considered an excellent instructor with very consistent, positive ratings from the students in his classes, he required the academic credentials in order to be able to teach the classes at a University.

When organizations hire people to do a certain job, they generally cannot afford the time or the risk of having people try out for a couple of months to see if they are competent. Instead, from all the applicants on file, they begin a winnowing process, starting with criteria that are both relevant (hopefully) and observable. This first criterion is often some sort of certificate or degree from a recognized post-secondary institution.

The thinking goes like this: "I have fifty people applying for a position, and I can select only one person. Many of them would probably be good, but I can't interview all fifty in order to select one. Forty of the applicants have a degree while ten do not. Therefore, the easiest thing to do in order to get the list down to the top four or five to interview will be to toss out the applications of those who do not have a degree. Might some of them be excellent employees? Sure, but I have to reduce the list from fifty to five, and I have to start somewhere."

The more senior you are in a position, the less likely it is that your job will actually require you to do the things you needed to be able to do to get qualified in the first place. But, without the credentials, you will lack the credibility required to direct those who do have that piece of paper.

The setting of a degree as an arbitrary standard makes sense for an organization when there is a large labour surplus and every job vacancy is met by five hundred applications. It makes it very difficult for the individual worker, however, who is faced with either returning to school or staying at a plateau.

Many people don't go back to college or university, even on a part-time basis, because of fear. They are afraid that they aren't smart enough, that they will look silly, or that they can't afford to go. There are many ways of getting post-secondary training today and not all of them demand that you go back to school full-time. Many post-secondary institutions are offering degrees online, by correspondence, or through work-study combinations where it is not necessary to quit your job and be a full-time student.

For those of you who still have nightmares about high school, it's helpful to know that there is not a lot of resemblance between today's adult education courses and the classes you remember from high school. Your classmates are generally supportive, people value experience as much as they do theory, and the curriculum is usually designed to reflect the world of the adult learner. Plus, if you have a major disinterest or lack of ability in a particular area it is often possible to obtain a degree without ever having to take a course in that subject. In the early 70s when I looked at obtaining a master's degree, I enrolled at Fordham University in New York City. There were two reasons for this choice. The first one was that I wanted the opportunity to live in a completely different environment from that which I had experienced to date. And second, to be honest, was that I needed to find a graduate school that did not require competence in a second language as part of the admission process. Canadian university graduate programs at that time all required an ability to read a second language. My ability to read French was limited to part of the back of cereal boxes.

TO DO

Talk to people who are now doing the job that you want to do. Find out how their career path led them to this position and what kind of training and experience they suggest you need.

Talk with a counsellor at a post-secondary institution and see what qualifications you need in order to be accepted as a student. Different institutions have different entry requirements. Look at online programs that are becoming more widely available. Much of the preliminary work can be done via the Internet with respect to programs, qualifications for admission, costs, and courses.

Remember that you get there one course at a time. Twenty courses appear pretty daunting. One course per semester may be manageable.

If you haven't been back at school for a number of years, try a not-for-credit short course offered by most post-secondary institutions. This will have the benefit of easing you back in slowly to the academic world while presenting an environment where your work experience will be valued. You may have more specific industry experience than the instructor. And at the end of it all you will have developed not only a larger knowledge base, but also something even more important. You will have developed the satisfaction that comes from having attempted and succeeded at something that you found challenging.

R
IS FOR RAISES

I have enough money to last me the rest of my life unless I buy something.
— Jackie Mason

JASON TILTED BACK ON HIS chair, in danger, Julia thought, of toppling completely over. They were relaxing in Julia's office before booking off for the Christmas break. There wasn't much business being done on this day, although there was a high noise level as staff wished one another season's greetings and made preparations to leave for the holidays.

"So, Jule," Jason said as he continued to balance precariously on two legs of the chair. "What are you going to spend your raise on?"

"I'd prefer Julia, if you don't mind, Jason."

"Okay, whatever. Anyway, I've got holiday plans and the extra money will cover them. Christmas at a great ski resort. My girlfriend and I are leaving tonight and should be on the slopes tomorrow morning. It's going to be pricey—first-class all the way, but the raise plus the Christmas bonus will cover all of it."

"Bonus and raise?" asked Julia, her eyebrows going up.

"Well, sure," replied Jason, oblivious to Julia's tone. "I went into Tom with a list of everything I had done this last year and told him that I deserved a raise for all the extra work I had done and the additional accounts that I brought in. He agreed. Simple. As a matter of fact, when he saw my list, he even made a change to the bonus I was getting. Phoned Lori right when I was in the office and told her to up it by five per cent more. Boy, I love this company! You get results and you get rewarded.

"So," he went on, "what are you going to spend all your extra money on, Jule, er, Julia?" he corrected.

"Probably on a get-well card for you if you fall off the ski-lift and bash your head on a snow bank. Now, if you'll excuse me, Jason, I have to go and wish Tom Merry Christmas and one or two other things." She got up abruptly and left her office, leaving Jason to wonder if he perhaps should not have said anything about the raise.

TO THINK ABOUT

Many workers operate under the somewhat naive assumption that if they work hard they will be recognized and rewarded, especially by receiving a raise. In this age of entitlement, many employees think that they "deserve" a raise simply for showing up and coming to work every day.

The whole issue of compensation is complex and often mired in secrecy. People who have no hesitation in telling you all about their sex lives will draw back in horror if you were to enquire about the amount of money they make.

Many workers operate in a work environment where raises are given to the bold, and not necessarily the good. It can at times be the business version of "the squeaky wheel getting the grease." The fact is that unless you are working in a modern, well-managed organization with a progressive and competent HR department, the amount of money you make and the raises you receive will have as much to do with your ability to demand what you think you are worth as it will with your ability to do the work.

There are times when it is smart to ask for a raise and times when it is suicidal to try the same manoeuvre. Obviously, if the company has just posted its third successive quarterly loss, then that is not the best time to look for increased compensation.

First of all, you need to know why you are asking for a raise. Is it because you can't make ends meet on your income? That may well be true, but most employers don't consider that to be their problem. Nor do you ask for a raise because there is going to be an addition to your family or because the guy next to you got one.

Look at the quality of your work. What have you done lately that warrants an increase in income? If you don't know, how do you expect your boss to understand that you are worth more?

A raise should reflect the value of your work, your contributions, your increased knowledge, and your experience. If these things have happened—that is, you do know more, you are doing better work, faster, more of it more efficiently, and your work output shows this—then your value to the company has increased and it is legitimate to think that this will be acknowledged and recognized by a raise in base salary.

TO DO

Keep your own file folder with information about what you have completed each month. Identify all projects and tasks—especially things that are not covered by your job description. Focus on what you achieved and what benefit it was to the company.

Keep track of all reading, courses and things that you have learned on your own that contribute to making you more productive and of more value to your company.

If you can, find out what other people in comparable positions in your company are making. If this is not possible, then find out what people in similar positions in your industry are making in your part of the country. Government agencies such as the Department of Labour frequently publish salary data by type of company and size. If you are being paid significantly less, then prepare your case for a raise.

This is not to suggest that you march into your boss's office and demand a raise or else you are gone. Make sure you never threaten to leave unless you have another job waiting. (This is different than not leaving unless you have another job waiting. Sometimes you have to leave a bad job, even if there is nothing else you can step into immediately).

What do you do if your boss puts you off and says that there isn't any money for raises? Do you meekly accept that pronouncement and go back to your desk with your tail between your legs or do you continue to negotiate when and how a raise might eventually be forthcoming? Determine when the next raise is planned and that your boss anticipates that you will be receiving one. In the meantime, you might want to angle for a change in job title—this can be beneficial if you have to look for another job. Take some additional courses or training if there is money in the training budget or even negotiate some additional time off. Remember, everything is negotiable, especially the amount of money you earn.

S
IS FOR SEX

> *Sex: the thing that takes up the least amount of time and causes the most amount of trouble.*
> — *John Barrymore*

"TOM, YOU REMEMBER TIFFANY?" ASKED Lori as she met Tom in the hall.

"Ah, yes, I think I do. Wasn't she the girl you had problems with regarding her lateness?"

"Woman," corrected Lori automatically. "And no, that was Amanda. Tiffany came on as a junior clerk is the HR Department. Her performance has been quite strong, so when an opening came up in Frank's area, I supported her application for that position. She got the job of course—she's very personable, and evidently Frank thought so too."

"So what's the problem?"

"Well," she hesitated. 'Can we talk about this in your office?"

They walked down the hall to Tom's office and Lori took a chair by the coffee table in the corner. Tom closed the door behind him and sat down in the chair across from her.

"Now, what's up with our pretty little Tiffany?"

"You're not the only male in the company who has noticed that Tiffany is young and attractive, Tom, and that's the problem."

"Problem? It's a problem that we have good looking girls, er, young women in the company?"

"No, being attractive is not a problem. But having an affair with a married man who is also her boss, is a problem," Lori said in a tone that sounded less judgemental than she felt.

"Whoa, that's a pretty serious allegation, Lori. How do you know that she's just not flirting with Frank, and just using her charms to get along in the new job?"

"She's using her charms all right. My admin had been spending a lot of her time away from her desk lately, taking longer than usual coffee breaks and longer lunches. I finally asked her if there was anything wrong, or if I could help in some way. She told me that Tiffany told her that she and Frank were having a 'fling thing' and that Frank's wife found out and now she was calling Tiffany at work and crying hysterically. Tiffany told her that nothing was going on between her and Frank, but Frank's wife keeps calling and trying to check up on them. All the clerical staff in the office know about this and they spend an inordinate amount of time gossiping about it."

"Maybe we should just remind them about our values of not gossiping," suggested Tom.

"Tom," Lori said heatedly, "you need to take this seriously. Frank is twice the age of Tiffany and he's her boss, and we're potentially liable for a sexual harassment suit, especially since Frank has a reputation for this sort of thing."

"Oh, Frank doesn't mean anything wrong. He's just a good ol' boy who likes to make pretty young women feel special. He says it gets them to work harder. But," he continued, seeing the look on Lori's face, "I will talk to him. I suppose we could always transfer Tiffany down to the records division, or over to computer support. Those guys are such geeks that they probably won't even notice a new clerk down there."

"Tom, you can't demote Tiffany and just move her to another area. And we can't appear to condone the actions of a senior member of the management team when they clearly violate our own policy not to mention legislation."

"Well, Lori, you're the HR Manager. You decide how to best deal with it. That's why we pay you the big bucks." He got up to indicate that the conversation was finished.

TO THINK ABOUT

And now for that part of the book that everyone reads first.

As far as sex in the office and office romances go, the old double standard works again. Men are penalized far less often for engaging in an office romance while woman seldom come out winners.

Office romances create numerous problems in organizations. First of all, there is the lost productivity as those who are engaged in the romance spend time communicating with each other, dreaming about each other, writing notes, texting, spending long lunches, extended coffee breaks, and so on.

It is amazing how quickly people find out about office romances. The participants think they are being so careful, so casual, so unobtrusive, yet everyone else sees exactly what is happening. That creates the next problem surrounding office romances—not only does the involved couple's productivity go down, but the rest of the staff lose work time as they discuss among themselves the budding romance.

If one of the partners in the office romance is married, additional gossip is created, and once the married partner finds out and phone calls or visits begin to the office to confront the "other woman," then severe problems and consequences develop.

It is difficult to avoid sexual attraction in the office environment. Work has all of the attraction and few of the limitations of home: intellectual stimulation, adult conversation, no kids, spilled milk, or garbage to be taken out, or home improvements to be sandwiched in after fighting traffic for an hour on the way home.

Whenever men and women work together the issue of personal attraction and the possibility of personal sexual attraction exist. People are, at their core, sexual beings, and to deny this rather elementary fact is to set yourself up for a potential disaster. People may make decisions about avoiding sexual involvement for a variety of reasons, but to think that working people would never develop a sexual attraction is naiveté of the highest order.

Sex in the office is not a moral issue, but it can be a career issue.

TO DO

Love may be blind but your colleagues aren't. Seldom is an office romance or affair unknown to co-workers. Office affairs can almost never be kept secret. If you don't mind being the target of office gossip and of having any recognition or promotion judged as being based on your horizontal activity, then by all means continue the relationship. If you have any concerns about your career, however, it is better to keep your sex life out of the office.

If you engage in a sexual relationship with someone in your company who has a less senior position than you do, you could be subject to charges of sexual harassment, especially if the person is a direct report. This is more likely to happen when the affair cools (as it frequently does), even when the relationship is consensual.

If your company does not have a policy on sexual harassment, it should have one. Every state and province has legislation regarding this issue. Contact the appropriate body for information about employer responsibilities concerning this topic.

If you are having an affair with your boss, it will end badly—most often for the person in the subordinate position. If you find yourself involved in an office romance, start looking for other areas in the company to work in, or start sending out your résumé. You may as well get a head start on the inevitable.

T
IS FOR TEAMWORK

Teamwork is everybody doing what I tell them to do.
— *Anonymous*

TOM LOOKED AROUND AT HIS management team. They were a team in theory he thought, but in reality they were a group of individuals. They didn't seem to have much in common outside the office, unlike the old days when there was him, and Frank, and…. He stopped. There was no one left of the old, original team. He and Frank had been the youngest and had grown up in the company. And one by one the older members had retired, or died, only to be replaced by others until finally he was at the top, and Frank was now his most senior management team member.

The original team had lots to do with one another, inside and outside the office. They had a company baseball team in the spring and summer, and played flag football in an industrial league during the fall. They would spend weekends helping one another build their decks or pour cement for a new driveway. Their wives were friends too, and would spend time together sitting beside the pool watching the kids while the men stood around the barbecue, beers in hand, and argued over the merits of their favorite baseball team, or the best strategy to increase market share for the company.

He was sure that all the out-of-office socializing went a long way toward building a more effective management team in the office. But now they seemed to have so little in common. Not everyone was married, and those that were were either empty nesters like himself and Frank, or else childless like Lori. One of them was even a vegetarian, for heaven's sake. None of them played any team sports or did anything they could all do as a group. Jason skied in the winter and ran half-marathons during the spring and summer; Lori said she walked her dog. He and Frank golfed together once a week, but he doubted whether Norman did anything athletic. Karim played video games, of course, and was working on a new game that he hoped he would be able to sell. And Julia said that she got her exercise running up stairs and jumping to conclusions. He shook his head. She was kidding, he hoped.

"Okay, people," he began as everyone settled into their chairs around the boardroom table. "I'd like Jason to start by sharing an idea he has for a new project for the company. It will demand a lot of time and effort and cooperation from all of you, but I know you're all up for it, and the rewards could be substantial."

'Yeah," whispered Julia to Lori, "the rewards for Jason will be substantial because you gotta know that it's his idea and he'll be taking all the credit."

TO THINK ABOUT

Some people like teams only if they are the team leaders. They don't make good team members. They spend so much time and energy jockeying for position and control that they either split the team or render it dysfunctional. Others like playing on a team so long as it is a winning team and they are having fun. Once it begins to lose or falter, they jump off the bandwagon and find another team to support. A few people hate teams because no one wants to work as hard as they do or meet the same standard of excellence.

And finally, there are those who are the true team players. They hang in forever, are loyal to their team and support it, win or lose.

If there is one inescapable reality about the modern workplace it is that everyone is expected to know how to be a good team player. Few managers today can possibly know everything she or he needs to know to make a good decision. Presidents and CEOs depend on expert advice and counsel from their legal staff, computer experts, financial specialists, and HR professionals, among others.

At senior levels in organizations it is not uncommon to see the executive teams organized along functional lines, with each member responsible for her or his own silo. Frequently more energy is spent trying to outdo their fellow executives than on trying to beat the competition. In many cases, their fellow executives are the competition.

In good functioning teams, people understand their roles, have common goals and know how their roles and effort contribute to the achievement of their goals. There is an understanding and acceptance that individual needs must, at times, be subordinated to the need of the entire group.

A senior oil and gas executive gave me his definition of being a good team player. "Before a decision has been made," he said, "we want input from everybody. We need ideas that support and cautions about what might go wrong. People should speak out forcefully and passionately. However," he continued, "once the decision has been made as to our goal, you are either on the bus or off it. You need to stop fighting against something you don't like, and work at making the plan work. If you can't do that, then you're not a team player."

TO DO

Team members support one another, and that means nobody trashes team members outside the group. In public, be supportive of the rest of your team. Don't criticize and don't complain. Team members have fun together as well as work together. What are you doing to do to bring some humour and fun into the team?

Members of good, functioning teams will often disagree in an effort to create the best solutions, but they do so in a way that values their colleagues' ideas and suggestions. There is mutual respect for the contributions of all.

Men and women often have different ideas as to their understanding of what being a good team player looks like. Women frequently think that a good team player is someone who looks around, sees what has to be done, and offers to help out without having to be asked. Men often describe a good team player as someone who plays his role effectively and doesn't need someone to come over and help out. Many men interpret an offer of help as a criticism of their ability to do their job; not offering to help is interpreted by many women as selfish and lazy. The first task of a new team, then, will be to discuss and set expectations around the whole idea of what a good team player looks like.

If you have the responsibility of being a team leader, the first key element to work on is to ensure that everyone is clear about the goal. Once goal clarity has been achieved, focus on establishing the required team roles and ensuring that everyone is aware that successful completion of the goal requires the cooperation of all team members. Too often when teams fail to achieve a goal, one or more members of the team absolve themselves of any responsibility by proclaiming that "they did their part right." If you hear that, then you know you have a collection of individuals pretending to be a team.

U
IS FOR UNCERTAINTY

Life's uncertain – eat dessert first.
— *Anonymous*

TOM BEGAN THE MEETING. "I'VE asked you all to my office first thing this morning to get your ideas on something that has just come up. I've just been made aware of a new opportunity for us to get brand new office space at a particularly favourable rate, and before I make my decision I'd like to hear about the implications that a move might have on your operations, especially if we do this within the next month."

"Sounds as if you've already made up your mind, Tom," said Julia.

"Not absolutely, Julia," replied Tom calmly, "but it is an outstanding opportunity that I think we should not overlook just because the topic hasn't been on our agenda this past year. If you're asking 'have I signed any papers?' the answer is 'no.' So, I am asking if there is anything that I should be aware of that would make 'yes' and not 'no' a better answer."

"What is it that makes this new building so terrific?" asked Frank. "Location, space, cost, proximity to the golf course?"

"The biggest advantage that this new space has, I think," said Tom, "is that it will double our current space without costing us any more than what we are paying now. If we decide to go ahead with our new marketing plans and bring on those couple of additional services, I can see us being much busier eight months from now. The additional space will allow us to bring all the new personnel we require and be an upgraded space to boot."

"But Tom," interjected Norman. "We haven't even made the decision to add those additional services. We still have a process that we are going through to make a business case for them and it's not certain yet that the case will be good enough for us to go ahead."

"When things often look too good to be true they often are too good to be true. What's the catch, Tom?" asked Lori.

'I don't think there is any 'catch' as you put it, Lori," Tom went on. "But there may be one drawback."

"Ha, now we get to the heart of the matter," said Julia. 'And what kind of catch, exactly, would this be?"

"Location," said Tom matter-of-factly. "It a new building in a new industrial park that is now being constructed just outside the city limits. That's one of the reasons why the price is so great. The owners are trying to attract new business and fill the buildings. They figure if the buildings are there, then the city will be forced to add transit and road improvements, and that other businesses will follow. They're betting on the city expanding to the north, so this makes it a perfect place. But, until the city does expand the transit, it means that people will have to have their own transportation to get to work. Jason," he went on, "you've been uncustomarily quiet. What impact would a move have on your area?"

"Oh, my people can work anywhere, Tom, but I've been thinking of some opportunities here for us. Will we get our name on the building? And will the building be visible from the highway?"

'Tom," said Lori slowly, "I know you asked about the impact on our staff. You know that the vast majority of the people in my area are clerical people and take city transit to work. I'm not sure how many of them would be able to find rides out to a new site, especially one so far away from where most of them live. And if we lose the staff that do payroll, then the impact could be quite negative on our entire operation, at least in the short run."

"Well, we wouldn't move everyone right away. Perhaps we could leave HR in this office," Tom replied.

"So it sounds like you want to move the head office people, except for HR, out to the new area in the new space, and leave the operations people here in this building," said Julia slowly. "It sounds like we are going to end up, then, with too much space in two buildings instead of just enough space in one building but no room for expansion here. Have I got that right?"

"Well, remember," said Tom somewhat defensively, "we might be expanding the services we offer."

"But that's not for certain, is it?" asked Norman.

"Norman, nothing is certain but death and taxes." Tom looked around the room. "Now, if there are no additional compelling reasons why we shouldn't seize this opportunity, I'll get on the phone and make this happen."

TO THINK ABOUT

There is probably nothing we can be more certain of than the fact that life is uncertain. The best we can hope for is to "guestimate" the probability of something occurring. We are surrounded by numbers, all purporting to predict the future. The weatherman predicts a sixty per cent chance of rain. Should we carry an umbrella or not? The sports caster announces that the home team is a five to one underdog. Should we lay down a bet with our neighbourhood bookie? Our company announces that it is going to lay off fifteen per cent of the workforce. Do we get our résumé updated?

There are people who are afraid of nothing and never appear uncertain, and there are those who are afraid of and appear uncertain about everything. The former handles uncertainty by jumping in immediately while the latter delays action as long as possible.

Is one approach better than the other? It might appear that in these days of high change that the person who is able to respond quickly in the face of uncertainty would have an advantage. This is true, if the actions taken are based on successful past experience and calculated risk tasking as opposed to acting because waiting is too stressful.

"I just have to act, to do something—anything," a manager told me. "If I don't, I get all stressed out and create all sorts of awful catastrophic scenarios in my head. It's better just to take some action and get it over with. If it works, great. If it doesn't, well then, you just try something else. At least you haven't wasted your time sitting doing nothing except worrying."

Some people seem to find it quite easy to act in the face of uncertainty. Part of their personal makeup includes a comfort level with uncertainty, and a strong enough ego to approach a risky situation and believe that by force of character or intelligence they can achieve success.

This is not an unmixed blessing. What might appear as unbounded confidence to others could, in fact, merely be a demonstration of anxiety caused by uncertainty. Having the patience to wait and see what develops rather than rushing in (even with the confidence that you can handle what is there) is often the smarter route to take. The ability to handle uncertainty does not mean that you jump in right away but that you have the courage to wait until the best time to act—wait for the best price, the best time, the best situation.

Creative people, as opposed to those who are less creative, differ in how they approach problem solving. Less creative people jump right into the problem and try to look for a good solution. Creative people seem to be able to tolerate the ambiguity that surrounds unresolved problems, and rather than starting with the potential solutions, spend much more time looking at, and redefining the problem. They seem to not to need to reduce their anxiety through achieving closure. Their capacity to live with the uncertainty that surrounds any new or difficult situation allows them to examine more permutations and combinations before arriving at a conclusion.

Some people have the motto, "Ready, fire, aim…oops." These are the "Impulsives" as opposed to the "Reflectives." The Impulsives appear to have less ability to tolerate ambiguity. They look around for the first solution that seems to fit and go for it, not even stopping to examine whether there might be an even better solution, or whether potential risks could outweigh potential gains. The Reflectives, on the other hand, look at many options, conduct risk analyses, and consult with others prior to making decisions or taking action.

Appropriate response to uncertainty presents a paradox for which there is no "right" answer. Act too quickly in the face of uncertainty and you will either succeed or fail; act too slowly in the same situation and you will either succeed or fail. The key is to know your own personal tendency to either be Impulsive or Reflective.

TO DO

If you are an Impulsive, ask yourself if you are taking action because you can't stand to wait and gather more information. If that is the case, take a deep breath, slow down and wait for more data. Ask yourself what the consequences of a bad decision are, and if they are too high, then force yourself to look for additional options.

If you are a Reflective, ask yourself if you are avoiding taking action because it is too risky, and too uncertain. If this is the case, identify what is the worst that could happen if you were to act now. Remember that you will never have all the information you think you need.

For both styles, it is very useful to create a chart that will outline what you know for a fact (data), what you think, based on experience, is likely to happen (and what level of confidence you have in this prediction), and what you are concerned about (but have no data to be able to predict with any accuracy). For items that appear in the last category, prepare a plan that would address how you would handle these concerns if they were to occur. Focus on managing the risks that accompany uncertainty and you will be able to act as needed when needed.

V

IS FOR VISION

Leadership is the capacity to translate vision into reality.
— *Warren Bennis*

"JASON," ASKED TOM, "WHAT DO you want to be when you grow up?"

"You mean besides rich and famous?" grinned Jason.

"No, I mean seriously. You're a bright young guy. You've got the credentials, that magic piece of paper. This is your first management job, but I'm sure that you will be looking for greener pastures pretty soon. You're pretty ambitious—and that's a good thing" he added hastily.

"So, is the famous 'Tom-fires-folks' talk that I'm getting?" asked Jason with a smile that was not quite as wide as it had been previously.

"No, no. That's not my intention at all, Jason. We're all, or at least I am, very happy with the work you have done in the six months since you've arrived. But we're a small company, and I worry that we are not giving you enough challenge to keep you happy—or productive."

"Well, this last six months has been fun and exciting," admitted Jason, "that's for sure. The company went from two sales reps to a full marketing and sales department and tripled the number of sales people. I think we're well on our way to moving from the small minor player position to a major, influential position in this area, and maybe not too long down the road, even to a national player spot." Jason leaned forward in his chair. "In fact, I can see us being a leader in the industry if we manage everything right."

"So, that's your goal, is it then, Jason, to be the biggest and the best?"

"Well, sure. You're the president—isn't that what you want, too?"

"When I was your age, I probably did," said Tom slowly. "Then, as times got harder and I got older, I guess I figured out that what was most important was to just be able to stay in the business and survive. Besides, there's a lot less stress when you aren't always trying to climb over everybody to get to the top. We've got a solid company, loyal customers and good suppliers. I'd be happy if we could keep our position and continue as we're doing now."

Jason's face fell. "Well, maybe as you say, Tom, I'm young and ambitious. But I took this job because I thought I could make a positive contribution and really help this company grow. Now it sounds as if that isn't in your plans at all."

TO THINK ABOUT

Perhaps the clearest characteristic that distinguishes a leader from a manager is the sense of having a vision and the ability to communicate that vision to others.

A vision begins as a picture in your mind's eye of a preferred future. If things were perfect, what would it, the future, look like? When you look out into the future what do you see? Do you have a clear sense of what perfect looks like?

Your rational mind might jump in here and say, "It's impossible to know what the future holds, so why worry about it? Just handle things as they come."

That's not altogether a bad strategy, and can encourage a kind of flexibility in adapting to rapidly changing circumstances that can be quite useful. But it is not the strategy of a leader.

Leaders are people who have a very clear picture in their head as to what the future should look like. That vision drives their actions. Everything they do is done with the vision in mind, and what they do is designed to advance the attainment of that vision.

It is vision that gives the sense of excitement and vitality to a company. Vision provides the energy and focus that gives everyone, clients as well as customers, a clear sense of direction. Many companies may have a mission statement, often written in such turgid prose that scarcely anyone reads it let alone remembers it, but few people actually think that the company actually wants to achieve that mission.

So why do some people appear to have vision while others don't? Like creativity, I believe that everyone has vision to start with, but it is extinguished in most people as they grow up. There are demands to conform to and follow. Young people who challenge the system are punished or criticized. The rewards are reserved for those who fit in. A goal of trying to get what everyone else is trying to get is not a vision. A goal that does not demand that people somehow grow in their attempt to reach that goal is not a vision. A goal to tear down something without replacing it with something different is not a vision.

We fail ourselves and our society if all we do is promote critical thinking without promoting creative dreaming and visioning at the same time.

TO DO

How can you promote vision, both in yourself and others?

Take some quiet time for yourself and reflect on your earliest dreams and desires. What did you see yourself becoming and what was it that attracted you to that dream? Do you have the same kinds of dreams today?

What is your individual mission statement? Why are you here and what are you called to do? Can you write this down in one sentence?

When others complain about something, anything, listen to them, acknowledge their complaint, and then ask the critical question: If this were a perfect world, how do you think this situation would look? Then ask the follow-up question, which is, perhaps, just as important: What do you think you can do to bring this better situation about?

There is an exercise that is sometimes done in career planning workshops where participants are asked to write their obituaries as if they had died the day before. What would be in your obituary notice and would you be happy about what it said? Suppose your date of death is twenty-five years from now. What would you like to appear in your obituary then? That sense of what you want to be and where you want to go is the underpinning of any corporate vision. The difficult part is not getting people to buy into the vision, it's having the vision in the first place.

What vision do you give to your staff? What vision do you have for yourself? The results of a vision are always noticeable.

W
IS FOR WATER COOLER

A desk is a dangerous place from which to watch the world.
— *John LeCarre*

"SO, WHAT'S WITH JULIA? DOES she hate me or what?" Jason asked Lori as they ate lunch together in the company lunchroom. It was after one p.m. and they were the only people in the room.

"Good heavens," exclaimed Lori, "what make you think that she hates you, Jason?"

"Well, whenever she walks by this lunch room and sees me in here having a coffee with someone, she just looks annoyed and stomps off down the hall. And when I've asked her if she'd like to do lunch, she puts me off with some sort of comment about having too much to do to spend time taking an extended lunch hour. Geeze! You'd think that I suggested that we fly to Rome for pizza or something."

Lori looked down guiltily. Just yesterday she and Julia, or rather Julia, had been discussing Jason's "pathetic lack of work ethic so common among the young these days," to use Julia's words. "I don't think Julia hates you," Lori began slowly. "She's just very focused on her work, and perhaps doesn't think she has time to stop and chat. She has a lot on her plate, you know," she added somewhat defensively. After all, Julia was her friend; they had worked together for over ten years now, and Lori, to be truthful, agreed somewhat with Julia's feelings about Jason's work ethic.

"But how does she know what is going on with everybody if she doesn't stop and chat with people over coffee?" asked Jason. "It's the chit chat that goes on when we're not working that makes it easier to work with everyone when the job gets tough. Besides," he laughed, "what with our brand new water purification system? She doesn't even have to drink that terrible coffee we seem to like so much."

"I've often wondered how you younger folks can drink so much of that stuff," smiled Lori.

"Trust me, Lori, it's not the coffee. It's the conversation."

"But Jason, you talk to people all day. You're constantly talking to the people in your group about your marketing projects. I don't understand why you have to spend time chatting so much with others in the lunch room," blurted out Lori.

Jason looked at her shrewdly. "Sounds as if you think I'm not working very hard, Lori."

"It's not that, Jason," Lori protested quickly. "It's just that, well, I have noticed that you do seem to spend a lot of time in the lunch room having coffee, and engaging in chit chat, as you put it."

"Part of it is that I'm a social guy, for sure, Lori. But there's more to it than that. I don't see this as goofing off. I ask my people to work hard and put in long hours, and they do. But to get that kind of commitment I have to know them as people—what they like, what they do in their spare time, what their kids do, if they have dogs, or what's happening in their lives. If they know I am interested in them as an individual, not just as a worker bee, then we form the kind of relationship where people are willing to give of themselves when we need the extra effort. And maybe the biggest bonus of all is that I am really plugged in to what is going on in the company. I probably know what's happening in your area before you do, Lori." He smiled to show he was not criticizing her.

"Not only that," he went on, "other people stop in for coffee—people from other departments in the company. I get to know them, they get to know me. And it's amazing how that builds better inter-department cooperation. I get lots of things done just by knowing who to go to first.

"If Julia would just get off her high horse and condescend to have a real conversation with folks about something other than her workload, I bet she'd get a lot more help, too."

Lori couldn't resist a small jab. "Is that something they taught you at business school?" she asked.

Jason laughed. "Nope. Figured that one out all by myself. But it has paid big dividends at the previous two companies I've worked for. And Lori," he added as he got up to take his tray to the rack, "I'm not just Mr. Social. You might want to check the last performance management reviews. You'll see that I met all my goals, and implemented a couple of additional initiatives that were very effective." He winked at her and said over his shoulder as he walked off, "I call it 'getting results by hanging around the water cooler.'"

TO THINK ABOUT

For a while the water cooler seemed to disappear from the office environment. Instead, it was replaced by coffee machines, espresso makers, or cute little cappuccino machines. In the last few years with the emphasis on health, and the advent of bottled water, office water coolers have begun to make a comeback.

These devices, whether they dispense water or coffee, are important not because they provide a needed beverage but because they provide a meeting space for people to come together. It allows people to form a community and share information, fun, caring, and concern—all those things that people can do for one another but machines cannot.

Some people see hanging around the water cooler as an excuse to goof off, and yes, there are some people who find social interaction more fulfilling than their work. Given the makeup of some jobs, that's hardly surprising. However, the attitude that hanging around the water cooler is a waste of company time illustrates the model of man as machine—that he can be switched off and on.

People need a water cooler because people need people. The water cooler is the excuse that brings people together. The "holier-than-thou" attitude that says, "While you guys are goofing off out there, I'm in here working my fingers to the bone," also says loud and clear that you are not one of the team—that you don't have an interest in the others you work with as people.

TO DO

When you come to the office, say good morning to everyone.

Take some time every day to get out of your office, have a drink of water, coffee or juice with someone else in the office. Find out what is going on. Get plugged in to the grapevine.

Don't have coffee with the same people all the time. Spend some time, even if it's just a short, casual conversation, with everyone you work with.

If people talk about sports, then at least read the headlines in the sports page and know how the home team did. It won't kill you to learn about ballet, opera, or Zen, or the care and feeding of llamas for that matter.

Ensure that your water cooler conversations are not character assassination or bitch sessions.

X
IS FOR XANTIPPE

*I will name you the degrees. The first, the Retort Courteous;
the second, the Quip Modest; the third, the Reply Churlish;
the fourth, the Reproof Valiant; the fifth, the Countercheck Quarrelsome;
the sixth, the Lie with Circumstance; the seventh, the Lie Direct.*
— Shakespeare

"JULIA, PLEASE COME IN." TOM moved over toward the door and closed it behind her.

Julia moved toward the couch in the corner but stopped when she saw Tom moving back behind his desk. She walked over to the desk and sat in the chair in front of it.

"Julia, this is not going to be an easy conversation, so I'll just get to the point right away." Tom began. "We've had talks about staff complaints before, about your anger outbursts in public with them, and the difficulties you seem to experience with some of the other managers in working with them. I thought we had worked out a plan to address that."

Julia said nothing, but her jaw hardened and her eyes grew narrower.

Tom continued. "I've had two more complaints this week. Both Frank and Jason have come to me wondering how to handle you."

"Oh, so now Mr. Social and Mr. Girl-friend-In-Every-Office have complaints about how to handle me, do they? Maybe they should look to their own behaviour first. I'm sick and tired of being made the bad guy around here." She crossed her arms and glared at him.

"It's not just those concerns," said Tom, "although they are part of a pattern I see. The issue that made me decide to take some action was our last staff meeting and what happened during it."

"So I suppose you're blaming me for the shouting match. Honestly Tom, I cannot see why you continue to tolerate Jason and his laziness. He promises things and doesn't deliver, he spends all of his time in the coffee room laughing about whatever stupid sport was on TV over the weekend, and he undermines me with my own staff. At the last staff meeting I just called him on some behaviours that I find particularly annoying—something that you should have done weeks ago, by the way.

"And Frank! Don't get me started on Frank. He's just one of the good ol' boys around here, and sexist to boot. He thinks that just because he comes into my office and smiles at me that I'll do half of his work and all of mine. Well, it just doesn't work that way and the sooner he figures that out, the better off we'll all be."

"Julia, have you ever heard the old saying, 'You catch more flies with a spoonful of honey than a barrel of vinegar?' People complain to me that you're always in a bad mood. They never know how to approach you. No matter what they suggest it seems that you find something wrong with it. And if anybody suggests something that you don't like, it seems that the fight is on. Julia, I can't have this kind of behaviour. It's making our management team dysfunctional and our meetings far too stressful.

"So, I have decided to put you on a paid leave of absence for a month. I want you to think about your future here, and what you can do to make some changes. Our benefit plan will cover any psychological services you think would be helpful."

Tom stood up indicating that the meeting was concluded. "Julia, you are a bright, competent woman, and I know you run a tight ship in Operations. Your department is probably the most efficiently run one that we have. But the price that we pay for that is just too high. We have much higher than average turnover in your area, and the management team, as I said, is just not able to function as a team in the face of your constant criticism and temper when you don't get your own way. So, as I said, I want you to take a month off, talk to somebody about this problem, and we'll have a discussion on the first of next month about your future with the organization."

Julia stood up, looked at Tom, turned on her heel and strode toward the door. "We won't be having any more conversations, Tom, at least not with me. You will be having a conversation, however, with my lawyer." She slammed the door.

TO THINK ABOUT

Xantippe was the wife of Socrates. Her major claim to fame, such as it is, is that she was reported to be a notorious shrew. It's interesting that the dictionary definition of a shrew is that of a bad-tempered, quarrelsome woman. There doesn't appear to be a male equivalent.

There are both men and women who seem to have the combined qualities of being bad-tempered and quarrelsome. These are people who seem to pick fights and have a capacity for very sharp verbal remarks that are meant to wound.

It is a trait associated with women possibly because women often are not able to defend themselves physically against men due to a difference in strength. They can, however, defend themselves verbally, and as the old sports motto says, the best defence is a good offence. Perhaps quarrelsome, bad-tempered men get into fights physically while women get into fights verbally.

Some people don't need management—they need therapy. Some people who are bad-tempered stay that way because there are payoffs for being miserable.

The first payoff is that you get to do just your own work and nobody else's. Nobody asks bad-tempered, quarrelsome people to help out by lending a hand. Consequently, they go home at the end of the day with just their lunch bag in their hands. (Of course they take a lunch bag. You think anybody wants to invite them to go out to lunch?) The second payoff is that people are generally very nice to them so that they don't receive a tongue lashing when they make a mistake. People try to handle shrews with kid gloves.

The third payoff is that when shrews are pleasant and seem to be improving, everybody is so grateful for the change in behaviour that they become even nicer to the shrew than they were before.

TO DO

The Xantippes in an organization are miserable, unpleasant, and like a shrew that consumes far more than its weight each day in its food intake, use up a disproportionate amount of organization energy. A great deal of company time and energy is spent planning how to be strategic in order to get the shrew's cooperation.

If you have a Xantippe in your office, seriously consider how you might transfer him or her out. They are almost never indispensable to the business. While shrews do not frequently get promoted to managerial positions, they often do have powerful positions. They may be executive gatekeepers, such as secretaries or administrative assistants to powerful executives. They may be the only person in a critical function so that everyone else is forced to deal with them, despite their unpleasant personality. The key here is to remember that while the function may be critical, the individual who occupies that position is not. If they were run over by a beer truck tomorrow they could be replaced.

And if Xantippe is your boss? There are few things that can destroy your confidence more quickly than a negative, critical, nagging boss who constantly points out your errors and has something new to complain about every morning. Unless you are an applicant for the Martyr of the Year Award, try to get an in-house company transfer or update your résumé and look for a job elsewhere.

If that is not possible, then develop as thicker skin and laugh off their comments. It is almost never possible to turn a shrew into a hamster.

Y

IS FOR YOUTH

That is the great fallacy: the wisdom of old men.
They do not grow wise, they grow careful.
— Ernest Hemingway

"JASON," ASKED KARIM, "WHEN DO you think Frank is going to retire?"

"Why, are you going to apply for his job?"

"You never know, Jason, I just might. At least I would be able to bring some 19th century thinking into the area. You don't have to be an expert to see that what we're doing is way out of date."

"19th century?"

"Yeah. I've given up hoping for 21st century solutions. I'd just be happy if Frank realized that we have computers now instead of stone tablets."

"It can't be that bad, Karim. You designed that new dispatch system for Frank to use. Isn't it working?"

"It works fine," replied Karim bitterly. "It took me four months, half of it on my own time, to design that system. Frank keeps using the one he had before. Says it's faster for him to use and he doesn't make mistakes on it, and something about not being able to teach an old dog new tricks. And he keeps a paper copy of everything. So much for the paperless office idea. I'll tell you, Jason. I am really tired of working for such a backward organization. My equipment at home is way more advanced than the relics they expect me to use here. How can they expect me to do my work when I don't even have the latest computer software?"

"Well," replied Jason reasonably, "that's just Frank. The other managers are pretty progressive aren't they?"

"We'll see," said Karim gloomily. "The next project is to design an HR information system for Lori. She doesn't know much about computers either, except for word processing. I don't think they even had electric typewriters when she first started working."

"That's a little harsh, Karim."

"Maybe, but it's true. You look around you Jason. All the new progressive ideas in this company are coming from guys like you and me and some of the younger people who are just waiting to be given a chance to make some real changes for the better."

"There's more to running a successful company than just having the latest technology," objected Jason. "You have to be able to work with people, too. My computer skills aren't that great either, you know."

"Sure, but at least you are willing to try some new things, Jason, and you always come and ask me if you aren't sure how to get the kinds of reports you need off the system. You're at least a 20th century thinker!"

"Thank you, I think," laughed Jason. "But we both need to remember that this company was built up over twenty-five years through personal contacts. We have a great reputation for reliability and dependability. From our latest marketing survey, our customers tell us that reliability is still the number one requirement. And you have to admit, nobody knows the dispatching part of the business any better than Frank. He's a legend in the industry."

"Maybe, but what do we do when Frank retires and takes all that knowledge in his head with him? And all we have left is a system that only he understands and uses. How long will it be before we can't be reliable and dependable anymore? That's my concern."

"Mine, too, Karim," admitted Jason. "Mine too."

TO THINK ABOUT

There's nothing much wrong with youth that thirty years or so won't cure.

It is certainly obvious, even to North Americans who are not traditionally introspective, that to be old is to be awful. Our society, and even more so, business, does not revere the elderly. It appears, at least to the young, that there is little to be learned from those who are old. The older workers are blocking career paths, are slow to accept new technology, new ideas, and new ways of doing things.

It has been said that Rome fell because as a civilization it became decadent. I think Rome fell because as a civilization, it became old. And in becoming old it became less eager to exert the energy needed to conquer and maintain far-flung lands.

Many companies now are looking to replace older workers with younger workers, holding out enticing early retirement packages to lure the fifty-five-plusses out of the office and into who knows what. There may be a heavy price to pay for all this, and the price is that we run the risk of losing the group memory. The young benefit from the group memory since past experiences can help to guard against future mistakes. Group memory can also save time by keeping people from a needless reinvention of the wheel.

What is perhaps most important is that people remain young, not in years, obviously, but in outlook. The characteristics we tend to identify with the young—a capacity for risk, an ability to bounce back after failures, the attitude that everything is possible—those are the kinds of characteristics that we all had at one time. Do we still have them now? What happened the last time someone came up with a new idea? Maybe you found yourself saying, "Oh, we can't do that around here—it's never been done before," or, "we've always done it like this." Young people don't say things like that, and if they do, then they're really old people in smooth skin.

The best combination of all is the ability to combine youthful thinking with experience. Older people are often smarter than young people, not because they are more intelligent, but because they have had enough time to experience a wide variety of things. This, of course, is dependent upon having twenty-five years of experience and not one year of experience twenty-five times.

Once you have stopped experimenting with new ideas, new techniques, and new technologies you have become old, even if you're only twenty-five.

TO DO

Are you really old but wrapped in smooth, wrinkle free skin? Bite your tongue if you ever hear yourself saying, "Oh, I'm too old for that kind of stuff."

Have at least one friend younger than you, and if you are under thirty, have at least one friend who is over fifty.

Try new things. Experience instead of judging.

Ask younger members of the workforce for their opinions and listen to them. You don't have to implement everything they suggest; neither do you have to reject every idea.

And if you are a member of the Generation X or Millennium Generation the older people in your company are not your parents. They may resemble them in many respects, but they are not responsible for any bad parenting you might have had. Try not to punish them for the sins of your folks.

There will be some major differences in values and expectations among the different generational groups. Youth anticipates, age regrets.

Z

IS FOR ZOMBIE

If you don't think the dead come back to life you should be around here at quitting time.

— *Office graffiti*

"YOU WOULD HAVE THOUGHT I was talking to a brick wall." Frank took a practice swing at his ball as he and Tom prepared to tee off at their regular weekend time.

"Well, Norman doesn't often get excited or show much emotion, that's true," replied Tom, taking his driver out of the bag. "Frankly, after my conversation with Julia, I am glad for the change of pace."

"But I can never tell what he is thinking," protested Frank. "At least with Julia you always knew where you stood. You might not like the spot, but you sure knew where she stood on things and how she felt about your position. With Norman, I just can't tell. He looks at you but doesn't say anything. I feel like asking him if anybody's home."

"Oh, I wouldn't advise that," Tom put in hurriedly, and then waited while Frank teed off. "I especially wouldn't let it affect your golf game," he added as the ball headed straight for a thick grove of trees.

Tom's shot followed the exact path of Frank's ball, so they moved down the fairway headed in the general direction of where the balls left the fairway.

"How did he ever get the job as CFO anyway, Tom?" Frank asked as he used his club to search for the ball among the tall grass surrounding the trees. "I don't recall seeing his résumé or knowing what his past work experience was."

Tom reddened slightly. "Well, our getting him was a little unusual. A friend of mine who does some teaching in finance at a private college recommended him. He got the highest mark ever given on the final exam. He said that if we wanted a really, really bright guy who could do miracles for us at the finance end we should snap him up. Of course, he's young and hasn't had any previous management experience, but then, the accounting folks pretty much manage themselves, I've always thought. But I must say that that he hasn't met my expectations."

"Didn't he fail one of his final exams?" asked Frank, lining up his shot from behind a rather large tree.

Tom waited until the shot bounced out onto the fairway before he replied. "Yes, and he was very upset. I told him not to worry about it, and just retake it, but I must admit being surprised that someone who was recommended as being at the top of the class would fail an exam. He did fine on the retake and now has all the official credentials required."

'Well, maybe he's qualified technically," said Frank as he watched Tom's shot go over the fairway and into the rough on the other side. "But he's a non-contributor. He doesn't say anything at management meetings and he doesn't seem to have any ideas or suggestions to offer. He just sits and takes up space. I would think that he's asleep except that his eyes are open."

"Technically his work is fine. He's accurate, gets things done on time. It's just that he is so, so, so not there. I had hoped for a little more leadership from him, but it doesn't look as if that's going to happen." He sighed. "I'll have a talk with him on Monday morning and see if I can't light a fire under him and get him to contribute more at meetings."

TO THINK ABOUT

Some people seem to have all the life of an overcooked noodle. They look limp, they talk limp, they act limp. It's not that they move slowly, it's more than there seems to be a severe energy drain. Some people are like emotional vacuum cleaners—they suck all the energy right out of you. You talk to them and you don't get any response. They look you in the eye (maybe) with no facial expression, and stare and stare and stare. You don't know if they like or dislike what you have said. You don't know if they have heard or not heard what you have said.

When these people come to seminars they don't laugh, nor do they groan. They don't applaud, hiss or boo. They don't look happy, or sad, or bored. That's just it. They don't look anything—they seem as lifeless as zombies.

What can you do if you have a zombie working for you?

TO DO

First, check your own expectations. What do you expect from them and do you have the right to expect it? You do have the right to expect that people will acknowledge that they have received a message; you might have to coach them on how to let you know that they have heard and understood what you've said, but you don't have the right to expect that they will be wildly enthusiastic about doing what you asked them to do.

Second, when speaking with them, try to ask them open-ended questions that will require them to elaborate on what they say rather than asking questions that they can answer with a simple "yes" or "no." Rather than asking "is that clear?" ask them to go over the steps they are going to take in order to get the project completed.

Third, don't expect these people to affirm you as a person, as a leader, or as a friend. They are incapable of positively affirming anybody. We all need support and positive affirmations from others about our abilities, ideas, and competencies. You won't get this from a zombie. On the plus side, you almost never find a zombie as a boss.

EPILOGUE

THE UNWRITTEN RULES ARE THE hardest ones to figure out. This is especially true when the rules were made by people who come from a different generation, perhaps with different values and certainly with different expectations.

The rules are unwritten not because anyone wants specifically to make your work life difficult, but because the people who make, or pass on, the rules think they are so obvious that they don't require any explanation or elaboration.

The situations that existed that gave rise to these rules may not even exist anymore. There is a story about a man who watched his wife prepare a Sunday roast and asked her, "Why do you always cut a slice off the end of the roast before you put it in the pan?"

"I don't know," she replied, "I guess that's how my mother always did it."

When they were next at his mother-in-law's house, he asked her, "Why did you always cut the end of the roast off before you put it in the pan?"

"That's a good question," she said. "Now that I think about it, I guess it's because that was how my mother showed me how to make it."

Fortunately granny was still alive, so the next time the husband saw her, he asked, "Granny, why did you always cut off the end the roast before you put it in the pan?"

"Because we never had a pan that was big enough."

Every business probably has rules, practices or processes that, at one time, made complete sense. And they linger even though the original reason for their introduction has long since vanished. In this way they are somewhat like some municipal bylaws regarding pedestrian right of way and horse traffic that have never been rescinded even though we seldom ride a horse down Main Street any more.

Some rules were embedded in the culture and country of the day. Contrast American informality in the use of first names with British or Dutch preference for the use of Mr. or Mrs., especially for those in senior positions.

The players in the little scenarios presented are no different from you or me or anyone else you work with. At one time or another they all broke rules—rules no one ever told them about until they transgressed. Some seemed to learn the lesson. Others? Not so much.

Perhaps some of these rules are in existence in your organization and your manager, older colleagues, HR or others just expect you to be aware of them. If so, and you have avoided some of the mistakes made by our fictional characters, then this volume will have served its purpose.

If not, then look for the unwritten rule that tripped you up in volume two.

CPSIA information can be obtained at www.ICGtesting.com
Printed in the USA
LVOW11s0824170315

430869LV00001B/10/P